SPECTRUM

Writing

Grade 6

Published by Spectrum®
an imprint of Carson-Dellosa Publishing LLC
Greensboro, NC

Spectrum® is an imprint of Carson-Dellosa Publishing.

Printed in the United States of America. All rights reserved. Except as permitted under the United States Copyright Act, no part of this publication may be reproduced or distributed in any form or by any means, or stored in a database or retrieval system, without prior written permission from the publisher, unless otherwise indicated. Spectrum® is an imprint of Carson-Dellosa Publishing. © 2015 Carson-Dellosa Publishing.

Send all inquiries to:
Carson-Dellosa Publishing
P.O. Box 35665
Greensboro, NC 27425

Printed in the USA
03-300147811

ISBN 978-1-4838-1201-4

Table of Contents Grade 6

Introduction

Chapter 1 Writing a Story

Chapter 2 Writing to Inform

Table of Contents, continued

Chapter 3 Writing an Argument

Introduction
Lesson 1 The Writing Process

Writers follow a plan when they write. They take certain steps, which make up the writing process. Following these five steps leads to better writing.

Step 1: Prewrite

This could also be called the "thinking and discovering" stage. Writers might choose a topic, or they might list everything they know about a topic already chosen. They might write down what they need to learn about a topic. Some also organize their ideas by making a chart or diagram.

Step 2: Draft

Writers put their ideas on paper. This first draft should contain sentences and paragraphs. Good writers follow their prewriting ideas while writing the draft. There might be spelling and grammar mistakes in this draft. There might even be mistakes in facts or ideas and how they are organized. That's okay; there are three more steps.

Step 3: Revise

Writers change or fix their first draft. They move ideas around, put them in a different order, or add new ones. They make sure they used clear words and the sentences flow smoothly together. This is also the time to take out ideas that are not on topic.

Step 4: Proofread

Writers usually write a neat, new copy. Then, they look again to make sure everything is correct. They look especially for capital letters, end marks, punctuation, and misspelled words.

Step 5: Publish

Finally, writers make a final copy that has no mistakes. They are now ready to share their writing. That might mean mailing a letter, turning in a report, or posting a story on a Web site.

Lesson 1 The Writing Process

What does the writing process look like? Chase used the writing process to write a paragraph about Sacagawea. His writing steps below are out of order. Label each step with a number and the name of the step.

Step ____: _____

Sacagawea was about 19 years old when she began traveling with Lewis and Clark on their great expeditoin. Her husband, a French fur trader named Charbonneau, had been hired as an interpreter. Though Sacagawea was "only a woman" and had a baby, she went along. Historians agree that Sacagawea's role in negotiating with her own Shoshone people aided the expedition a great deal so, it is Sacagawea, not her husband, who becomes a hero.

Step ____: _____

Sacagawea was about 19 years old when she began traveling with Lewis and Clark on their great expedition. Her husband, a French fur trader named Charbonneau, had been hired as an interpreter. Though Sacagawea was "only a woman" and had a baby, she went along. Historians agree that Sacagawea's role in negotiating with her own Shoshone people helped ensure the success of the expedition. So, it is Sacagawea, not her husband, who becomes a hero.

Step ____: _____
Shoshone
with Lewis and Clark, starting in 1805
carried her baby
husband, Charbonneau, interpreter
about 1786 to 1812

Step ____: _____

Sacagawea was about 19 years old, when she went with Lewis and Clark on their great expeditoin. Her husband, named Charbonneau, had been hired as an interpreter. Though Sacagawea was "only a woman" and had a baby, she went along Historians agree that Sacagawea's role in talking to her own Shoshone people aided the expedition a great deal, so, it is Sacagawea, not her husband, who becomes a hero.

Step ____: _____

Sacagawea was about 19 years old, when she went with Lewis and Clark on their great expeditoin. Her husband, named Charbonneau, had been hired as an interpreter. Though Sacagawea was "only a woman" and had a baby, she went along Historians agree that Sacagawea's role in talking to her own Shoshone people aided the expedition a great deal, so, it is Sacagawea, not her husband, who becomes a hero.

Lesson 2 Purposes for Writing

When you are in school, you write assignments for your teachers. Beyond completing a school assignment, though, there are several basic purposes, or reasons, for writing. In general, they are as follows:

- to entertain
- to persuade
- to explain
- to inform

Writers use many forms of writing, such as friendly letters, reports, news articles, book reviews, and poems. For one form of writing, there might be different purposes. Here are some examples.

Form of Writing	Possible Purposes
Personal narrative	To entertain, to explain
Story	To entertain
Friendly letter	To entertain, to persuade, to explain, to inform
Business letter	To inform, to persuade
Instructions	To explain
Letter to the editor	To inform, to persuade
News article	To inform, to entertain, to explain

Writers may combine purposes in one form of writing. For example, an article about knitting might be both entertaining and informative.

Below is a list of written products. Write what you think the purpose of each item is—to entertain, persuade, explain, and/or inform.

Written Products

a news article about a train wreck

a personal narrative about a tragic incident

a story about a girl and her dog

a business letter about a faulty product

Purposes for Writing

_____

_____

_____

_____

Lesson 3 Audience

When a children's author sits down to write a story, does he write a 112-page book? Of course not. His audience would not be interested in such a long book. A children's author must think about his audience and write especially for them.

Does the president of a company have to think about her audience if she is writing a memo to her employees? They are adults; they can understand anything. Right? Wrong. If she is going to keep their interest and get her message across, she needs to think about her audience just as much as the children's author had to think about his.

> Writers need to consider these questions every time they write.
>
> - What will my audience enjoy?
> - What are they interested in?
> - What will make them want to keep on reading?
> - What do they already know?
> - What will they understand?

Mr. Elkins, the gym teacher, has to go to a meeting tomorrow. He has written a set of instructions for the substitute teacher. Mr. Elkins knows that the substitute teacher has never taught a gym class before. Read the paragraph. Think about whether Mr. Elkins kept his audience in mind.

> After warm-ups, send the kids for two laps. Then, pick teams and have the fourth- and fifth-graders play dodge ball. The third-graders should play freeze tag. Set up all six centers for the first- and second-graders. Put the ball-bouncing center on the opposite side of the gym from the balancing center. Thanks and have a great day!

Lesson 3 Audience

Put yourself in Mr. Elkins's place and ask yourself the five questions on page 8. What else should Mr. Elkins have told the substitute teacher? Describe the sorts of things he should have included since he knew the substitute had never taught a gym class before.

_____

_____

_____

_____

Now, imagine that you are your own teacher. You also have a meeting tomorrow and must leave instructions for a substitute. What will the substitute need to make his or her way smoothly through the day? Remember, this substitute has never been in your classroom before. She knows the school's general schedule, but she doesn't know specific details about your class's schedule or about where things are in the room. Before you write your instructions here, ask yourself the five questions on page 8.

_____

_____

_____

_____

_____

_____

_____

_____

_____

_____

_____

_____

_____

_____

_____

_____

Lesson 4 Write a Paragraph

Here is what you know about paragraphs.

> - A paragraph is a group of sentences that are all about the same topic.
>
> - Each sentence in a paragraph stays on topic.
>
> - The main idea of a paragraph is what the paragraph is all about.
>
> - A paragraph's main idea is usually stated in a topic sentence. The topic sentence may fall anywhere in the paragraph.
>
> - The first line of a paragraph is indented.
>
> - Writers must consider the audience for which they are writing.

What is your idea of a perfect summer day? What would the weather be like? What would you do? Where would you be? List some details that would be part of your perfect summer day.

Details:

_____   _____

_____   _____

_____   _____

Review your list. Think about the order in which you want to present your details in a paragraph. If you wish, number them. Then, draft a paragraph about your idea of a perfect summer day.

_____

_____

_____

_____

_____

_____

_____

_____

_____

_____

Lesson 4 Write a Paragraph

Read through your paragraph. Ask yourself these questions. If necessary, make changes to your paragraph.

> ## Questions to Ask About a Paragraph
>
> **Does the topic sentence express the main idea?**
> **Does each sentence support the topic sentence?**
> **Does each sentence express a complete thought?**
> **Are the ideas and words in the paragraph appropriate for the audience?**
> **Is the first line indented?**

Now that you have thought about the content, or meaning, of your paragraph, proofread it for errors. Read through it several times, looking for a certain kind of error each time. Use this checklist.

_____ spelling   _____ end marks

_____ capitalization   _____ punctuation

Now, rewrite your paragraph. Use your neatest handwriting and make sure there are no errors in the final copy.

_____

_____

_____

_____

_____

_____

_____

_____

_____

_____

_____

_____

_____

_____

_____

_____

_____

Lesson 5 Main Ideas and Details

A paragraph has a main idea. The main idea is what the paragraph is all about. In most paragraphs, the main idea is actually stated in the paragraph. That statement is called the *topic sentence.* A topic sentence may be anywhere in a paragraph, but most often it is either the first sentence or the last.

In the paragraph below, the topic sentence is the first sentence. Write it below.

> My grandmother is one of those people who has her holiday shopping done by September. She picks out gifts when she and Grandpa travel. She also goes to local stores when they have sales during the summer. In December, when we're all feeling too busy, Grandma is at home baking cookies.

_____

_____

The other sentences include details that support, or tell about, the main idea. Write two details from the paragraph.

_____

_____

Lesson 5 Main Ideas and Details

Not all paragraphs have a topic sentence. Sometimes, writers leave it out. The paragraph still has a main idea, but the writer chooses not to state the main idea in the paragraph. That means the main idea is implied. Here is an example.

> All of the stores were crowded yesterday. They weren't necessarily full of people, though. Everywhere I went, there were special displays. I guess they figure that if you trip over the display, you're more likely to buy something. That's not how it worked for me. I was so annoyed that I cut my shopping trip short and went for a walk in the park.

What is the main idea of the paragraph above?

_____

How do you feel about shopping? Choose one of these sentences as a topic sentence for a paragraph:

I hate shopping.

I like shopping, but only for myself.

I would like to be a professional shopper.

Now, write a paragraph in which you support your main idea with details. Remember to choose just one topic sentence. Decide whether you will put it at the beginning, in the middle, or at the end of the paragraph.

_____

_____

_____

_____

_____

_____

_____

_____

_____

_____

_____

Lesson 6 Staying on Topic

Here is a good paragraph. It starts out with a topic sentence. Then, each sentence gives details about, or supports, the topic sentence.

> Many people say they would rather not live in a city, but few people actually make the move to the country. In a recent survey, 66% of the adults polled said they longed for a rural lifestyle. However, only about 2% of those people said they had actually taken steps toward such a move. Steps they had taken included searching for real estate and inquiring about job opportunities in rural communities.

The following paragraph contains a sentence that is not on topic. Read the paragraph and underline the topic sentence. Draw a line through the sentence that does not support the topic sentence. Then, list two details that do support the topic sentence.

> For a city kid, country life can be a little alarming. I learned that on a recent visit to see my aunt and uncle. As we pulled up in front of their house, a possum crossed the driveway. I let out a yell. I thought it was a huge rat! Possums are not even in the same family as rats. After we all settled down from that, my aunt's cat deposited a dead mouse on the doorstep. Aunt Terry calmly picked it up by the tail and tossed it into the bushes.

Detail: _____

Detail: _____

Now, write your own paragraph about an experience you have had in the country or outdoors. Remember to stay on topic. Stick to one main idea and make sure that all of your detail sentences support that main idea. When you are finished, underline your topic sentence.

_____

_____

_____

_____

_____

_____

_____

_____

Lesson 7 Active Voice

Usually, the subject of a sentence does the action. That is easy to see in this sentence:

Jason hung the picture.

The verb in the sentence is an active verb because the subject does the action.

What about this sentence?

The picture was hung.

First, is this a complete sentence? Yes, it is. It has a subject and a predicate. *Picture* is the subject of the sentence. Does the picture do the action? No, the picture does not do the action; the picture "receives" the action. The verb *was hung* is a passive verb because the subject does not do the action.

Passive verbs are always two-part verbs. There is always one of these helping *verbs—am, is, was, be, been*—plus a main verb. This does not mean that whenever you see one of those helping verbs, you are looking at a passive verb.

Passive verb: Jason was called upstairs.

Active verb: Jason was calling for help.

How can you tell the difference? Ask yourself these two questions:

What is the subject?

Is the subject doing the action?

If the answer to the second question is "yes," then you have an active verb. If the answer is "no," you have a passive verb.

Sometimes, you have to use passive verbs when you write. Maybe you don't know who did the action, so you have to write, "The picture was hung." Most of the time, however, your writing will be clearer and more interesting if you use active verbs.

Lesson 7 Active Voice

Compare these two paragraphs. The one on the left uses mostly passive verbs. The one on the right uses active verbs. What do you notice?

A grand opening was held last night by the art museum. A new exhibit was unveiled by the museum director. The collection of international textiles was assembled by Vince DiSilva. The textiles have been displayed previously by DiSilva in London and Los Angeles. The collection has been hailed by critics as the largest and most diverse of its kind.	The art museum held a grand opening last night. The museum director unveiled a new exhibit. Vince DiSilva assembled the collection of international textiles. DiSilva has displayed the textiles previously in London and Los Angeles. Critics have hailed the collection as the largest and most diverse of its kind.

Underline the subject of each sentence below. Put an **X** next to each sentence that contains a passive verb.

_____ Steve viewed the exhibit.

_____ The exhibit was lit with special lights.

_____ Elijah was looking at one display.

_____ Visitors were entertained by a pianist.

Practice writing sentences with active verbs. First, look at the sentences above that have passive verbs. Rewrite one of those sentences with an active verb.

_____

Now, write a new sentence about something that visitors might do at a museum. Make sure you use an active verb.

_____

Chapter 1

Lesson 1 Sensory Details

Scruunnch. I bit into my apple and juices flowed everywhere. At the same time, I felt some gooey brown caramel stick to my chin. I tried not to drool as I detached the bite of apple and got it all the way into my mouth. I had no napkin, wouldn't you know it, and had to fight the urge to wipe the sticky mess off on my white sleeve. I kept my head down so that no one would see the caramel hanging on my chin. I chewed quickly, though what I really wanted to do was savor the rich, sweet caramel blending with the tartness of the apple.

In a description, a writer's goal is to help readers see, hear, smell, feel, or taste what is being described. They use **sensory details**, or details that appeal to readers' senses, in their description. For example, in the paragraph above, *scruunnch* helps you hear the person biting the apple. The phrase "juices flowed everywhere" helps you feel what it's like to bite into the apple. What other sensory details does the paragraph contain? List them here, according to whether the detail helps you see, hear, smell, touch, or taste the caramel apple. Some details might fit into more than one category.

See: _____ _____ _____

Hear: _____ _____ _____

Smell: _____ _____ _____

Touch: _____ _____ _____

Taste: _____ _____ _____

Think about the last time you ate an apple. Was it covered in caramel? Maybe it was sliced up in a salad. How did it taste? What did it feel like? List the sensory details.

See: _____ _____ _____

Hear: _____ _____ _____

Smell: _____ _____ _____

Touch: _____ _____ _____

Taste: _____ _____ _____

Lesson 1 Sensory Details

Think of a food that you like. What is it like to eat that food? Imagine yourself eating and enjoying the food. Can you describe the experience so that a reader feels as if he or she is right there?

First, record the sights, sounds, smells, textures, and flavors you experience when you eat the food.

Sights: _____ _____ _____

Sounds: _____ _____ _____

Smells: _____ _____ _____

Textures: _____ _____ _____

Flavors: _____ _____ _____

Now, put your words to work. Describe what it is like to eat this food. Appeal to all five of your readers' senses. As you move between the senses, use transition words. Remember to indent the first sentence of your paragraph.

_____

_____

_____

_____

_____

_____

_____

_____

_____

_____

_____

_____

_____

_____

_____

_____

_____

_____

Lesson 2 Adjectives and Adverbs

To make a sentence, you need a noun and a verb. It takes just one of each to make a complete sentence.

Trucks rumble.

Adjectives and adverbs add description to a sentence.

> • An **adjective** is a word that describes a noun or pronoun. Adjectives tell *what kind, how much* or *how many*, and *which ones.* In other words, adjectives tell how things look, sound, smell, feel, and taste.
>
> • An **adverb** is a word that describes a verb, an adjective, or another adverb. Adverbs tell *how, when, where,* or *to what degree.* Many adverbs end in **ly**, but some do not, such as *not, never,* and *very.*

Adjectives at Work

Begin with a basic sentence and then notice how a few adjectives make it more interesting.

The trucks rumble down the street.

What kind of trucks are they? They are *huge* trucks.

How many trucks are there? There are *ten* of them.

What kind of street is it? It is a *bumpy* street.

Which trucks? It is *those* trucks.

Here is the new sentence. Notice that the adjectives go right before the nouns that they describe. This is almost always true. Doesn't this sentence make a more vivid image in your mind?

Those ten huge trucks rumble down the bumpy street.

Now, it is your turn. Look at the sentence below. Think of at least two adjectives to add to it, then write the new sentence. Remember, an adjective tells more about a noun or pronoun.

A driver blew his horn.

_____

_____

Lesson 2 Adjectives and Adverbs

Adverbs at Work

Start with the same basic sentence and see how some adverbs liven it up.

> The trucks rumble down the street.

When do the trucks rumble? They rumble *every day*.

How do they rumble? They rumble *noisily*.

Where do they rumble? They rumble *down the middle of the street*.

Here is the new sentence. Notice that one adverb comes several words before the verb it describes. The other falls right after the verb.

> Every day, the trucks rumble noisily down the middle of the street.

Look at each sentence below. Ask yourself whether you can add information about *how*, *when*, *where*, or *to what degree* with an adverb. Write your new sentence on the line.

A driver blows his horn.

_____

_____

The trucks roll to a stop at the corner.

_____

_____

Look at how both adjectives and adverbs work in this sentence.

young   proudly   shiny , new
The driver stood next to his truck.

Improve each sentence by adding one adjective and one adverb to make it more vivid.

The cab of a truck can be comfortable.

_____

_____

Trucks move goods across the country.

_____

_____

Lesson 3 Describing Objects

When a writer describes an object, readers should be able to see, hear, smell, feel, and perhaps taste it. Can you describe something so vividly that your readers feel as if they are right there seeing it or holding it?

Take a close look at a shoe. Look at it as if you are seeing it for the first time. Record its details here.

Color: _____

Shape: _____

Size: _____

Texture: _____

Smell: _____

Other details: _____

Now, write a paragraph in which you describe the shoe. Again, describe it as if you are not familiar with the object. Remember to appeal to as many of your readers' senses as you can.

_____

_____

_____

_____

_____

_____

_____

_____

_____

_____

_____

_____

_____

_____

_____

_____

_____

Lesson 3 Describing Objects

Now, try a more complex object, such as a backpack or book bag. Examine it. Even though it is a familiar object, look at it with fresh eyes. Record details of the object here.

Color:_____

Shape: _____

Size: _____

Texture: _____

Smell: _____

Other details:_____

Now, write a description of the object. Organize your details logically in a side-to-side or top-to-bottom format.

_____

_____

_____

_____

_____

_____

_____

_____

_____

_____

_____

_____

_____

_____

_____

Share your description with a friend, but don't tell what is being described. Can your friend guess what it is? Does he or she have any questions? Reread your paragraph and think about what your friend said. Is there anything you could do to make your writing better?

Lesson 4 The Writing Process: Descriptive Writing

Descriptive writing plays a role in many forms of writing. You see it in stories, in textbooks, and in newspaper articles. You can use the writing process to develop a paragraph that describes a setting of a story.

Prewrite

Suppose you are trying to describe a place to someone who has never seen it. It could be a hidden cave, a hideout in a tree, or even a space station. First, think of some places that you could describe thoroughly. List them here.

Places I could describe:

_____   _____

_____   _____

_____   _____

Now, look over your list. Which place do you think you can describe most vividly? Choose one and write the place that you decide on here.

Place I will describe: _____

Use this idea web to collect and record details about your place.

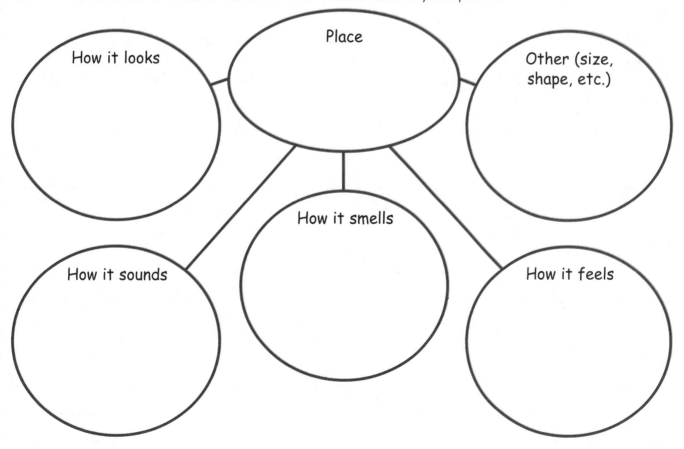

Lesson 4 The Writing Process: Descriptive Writing

As a final step in the prewriting stage, organize your ideas. How will you describe this place—from top to bottom? From side to side? Make a choice and record it here.

Method of organization: _____

Major details, in order:

Draft

Refer to your prewriting notes as you write a first draft here or in a computer document. Remember, this is the time to get your ideas down on paper in sentences. This is not the time to worry about getting every word just right. If you need more space, use a separate sheet of paper.

_____

_____

_____

_____

_____

_____

_____

_____

_____

_____

_____

_____

Lesson 4 The Writing Process: Descriptive Writing

Revise

All writers face the difficult task of reading what they have just written and trying to make it better. Reread your draft carefully. Will it be clear to your readers? Answer the questions below about your draft. If you answer "no" to any of these questions, then those areas might need improvement. Ask a friend to read your draft and answer the questions, too.

- Did you keep your audience in mind? Did you include details that will interest them and that they will understand?
- Did you organize your description in a logical way?
- Did you use adjectives and adverbs?
- Did you use vivid verbs and precise nouns to help readers see the place?
- Did you use sensory details? To how many of your readers' senses did you appeal?

Rewrite your description here or make changes to your computer document. Improve your message based on the questions you just answered.

_____

_____

_____

_____

_____

_____

_____

_____

_____

_____

_____

_____

_____

_____

_____

_____

Lesson 4 The Writing Process: Descriptive Writing

Proofread

Your description should be in good shape now. The last task is to check it for any remaining errors. It is best to read for one kind of error at a time. Proofread your revision on page 25. Use this checklist to help you catch all of the errors. Ask a friend to read your writing and answer the questions, too.

_____ Does each sentence begin with a capital letter?

_____ Does each sentence have an appropriate end mark?

_____ Are proper nouns (names of people, places, or things) capitalized?

_____ Are all words spelled correctly?

_____ Did you use commas correctly?

Publish

Write a final copy of your description here or make final changes to your computer document. Write or type carefully so there are no mistakes. Be careful not to introduce any new errors. Share your finished writing with someone who will enjoy it.

_____

_____

_____

_____

_____

_____

_____

_____

_____

_____

_____

_____

_____

_____

Lesson 5 Personal Narrative

Have you ever written a true story about something that happened to you? You were writing a personal narrative. A **personal narrative** is a true story a writer tells about his or her own experiences. Read Jana's personal narrative.

Perfect Hindsight

After school, I delivered the note to Dad, went up to my room, shut the door, and burst into tears. The note was from Mrs. Schrum, the school nurse. I hadn't read the note, but I knew what it said.

It said that I had been able to see hardly anything during the vision screening. Everyone else had read at least four lines of letters on the chart. I could see the big **E** at the top, though it was a little fuzzy. Then, I guessed at the letters in the second row. I felt so stupid.

A little later, Dad came up to my room. Dad wears glasses, but that doesn't matter because he's a dad. He told me that he was only in fourth grade when he got his glasses. That was supposed to make me feel better because I'm in sixth grade. I just kept crying.

It was several weeks before Mom was able to get me to the eye doctor. I pretended that the doctor would say there had been some mistake. "This girl can see perfectly fine," he would announce.

In fact, the doctor just said, "Hmmm. Mm-hmm." Then, as if it were no surprise, he sent my parents and me to pick out frames. I tried on about a million of them. It was kind of fun, actually.

A week later, the glasses were ready. I guess I had gotten used to the idea. I was kind of eager. As soon as they were on, I said, "Hey, wow." I could read a sign all the way across the street! I had had no idea the glasses would make such a huge difference. Then, I grinned up at my parents. "This girl can see perfectly fine," I announced.

Lesson 5 Personal Narrative

Here are the features of a personal narrative:

- It tells a story about something that happens in a writer's life.
- It is written in the first person, using words such as *I, me, mine,* and *my.*
- It uses time-order words to tell events in a sequence.
- It expresses the writer's personal feelings.
- It includes a good ending, or conclusion.

Some people write personal narratives because they want to share their thoughts and feelings. Some write because they want to entertain their readers. Some might want to do both. As always, writers of personal narratives keep their audience in mind. What do they want to share with those readers that would be of interest? Finally, personal narratives can be about anything that actually happens to the writer.

What could you write a personal narrative about? Look at these idea-starters.

a beloved grandparent	a funny uncle	the first day at a new school
an athletic feat (or failure)	a family trip	an illness in the family
an embarrassing moment	getting braces	

What memories popped into your head as you read these idea-starters? Jot some notes about each memory or another one that you think of. One of these could be the start of a great personal narrative.

Idea-starter: _____

_____

_____

Idea-starter: _____

_____

_____

Idea-starter: _____

_____

_____

Lesson 6 Sequence of Events

Los Angeles | New York | London | Paris | Tokyo

In a personal narrative, readers need to know when things happen and in what order. Understanding the order of events helps readers put other ideas together, such as why something happened or what meaning an event had. Think of all the time-order words or phrases you can and list them. The list is started for you.

after school	next year	fourth grade
Tuesday	sunrise	last month

Now, use some of the time-order words from the list above. Write a sentence that could be from a personal narrative. Use a time-order word or phrase at the beginning of your sentence to tell when something happened.

_____

_____

_____

Write a sentence about something you did yesterday. Use a time-order word or phrase in the middle or at the end of your sentence.

_____

_____

_____

Lesson 6 Sequence of Events

In addition to time-order words, transition words help readers know when things happen and in what order. Here are some common transition words.

after	as soon as	before	during	finally	first
later	meanwhile	next	soon	then	when

Here is a paragraph from Jana's personal narrative on page 27. Circle the transition words when you find them.

A week later, the glasses were ready. I guess I had gotten used to the idea. I was kind of eager. As soon as they were on, I said, "Hey, wow." I could read a sign all the way across the street! I had no idea the glasses would make such a huge difference. Then, I grinned up at my parents. "This girl can see perfectly fine," I announced.

Think about your morning routine. What do you do from the time you wake up until you get to school? Write this sequence of events in a paragraph. Remember that it is important to use transition and time-order words, but don't start every sentence with one. Use different sentence styles to keep your writing interesting.

_____

_____

_____

_____

_____

_____

_____

_____

_____

_____

_____

_____

_____

_____

_____

_____

Lesson 7 The Writing Process: Personal Narrative

Personal narratives can be about ordinary things. Remember the narrative you read on page 27? Jana wrote about getting glasses. Nothing dangerous or exciting happened. It was just an event in Jana's life, and it changed her a little bit. Follow the writing process to develop a personal narrative about an event in your own life. How did it change you?

Prewrite

Look again at the idea-starters on page 28 and the notes you made. Choose one of those ideas, or another idea that you like, and begin to explore it here.

My idea: _____

Use this idea web to collect and record details. Write down as many as you can.

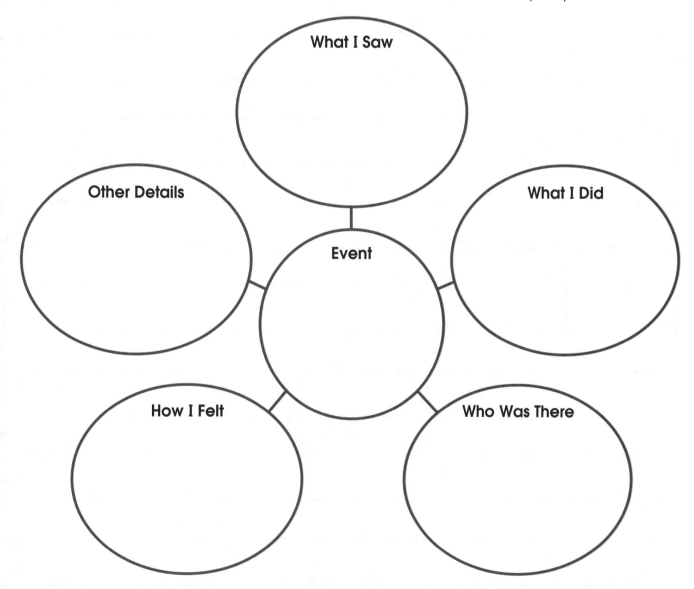

Lesson 7 The Writing Process: Personal Narrative

So far, you have chosen a topic and collected ideas. Now, it is time to put your ideas in order. Think about the story you are about to tell in your personal narrative. Use the sequence chart on this page to list the events in order. Don't worry about details here; just get the events down. Think about how you will conclude your story.

1. _____

↓

2. _____

↓

3. _____

↓

4. _____

↓

5. _____

↓

6. _____

↓

7. _____

↓

8. _____

↓

9. _____

Lesson 7 The Writing Process: Personal Narrative

Draft

Write the first draft of your personal narrative here or in a computer document. Look back at your sequence chart on page 32 to keep yourself on track. Continue on another sheet of paper if you need to. As you write, don't worry about getting every word just right. Get your ideas down in sentences and in order.

_____

_____

_____

_____

_____

_____

_____

_____

_____

_____

_____

_____

_____

_____

_____

_____

_____

_____

_____

_____

_____

Now that you have written your draft, write an idea for a title here.

Title: _____

Lesson 7 The Writing Process: Personal Narrative

Revise

One of the hardest things for any writer to do is to "fix" or change his or her own work. Writers put thought and effort into their work. It's hard not to read even a first draft and say, "Well, that's great." Good writers know that they can almost always improve their first drafts. Improve your own first draft by answering the questions below. If you answer "no" to any questions, those are the areas that might need improvement. Make notes on your draft about changes you might make later. Ask a friend to read your draft and answer the questions, too.

- Did you tell about just one event or one "thing" in your narrative?

- Did you include details to make readers feel as if they are right there with you?

- Did you tell events in order? Did you use transition and time-order words to show when events happened?

- Did you tell how you felt about the event? Do readers get a sense of your personal feelings?

- Did you use active verbs?

- Does your story flow smoothly when you read it out loud?

- Do you have a good conclusion that wraps up the narrative?

Now, focus on making sure you included details that will keep your readers interested. Did you use fantastic descriptive words, vivid verbs, and precise nouns?

When Jana revised her personal narrative, she replaced some overused verbs with more interesting ones. She also added the describing word *school* to help readers know what is happening. Here is how Jana changed the opening paragraph of her personal narrative.

       After school, I ~~gave~~ delivered the note to Dad, went up to my room, shut the door, and ~~cried~~ burst into tears. The note was from Mrs. Schrum, the school nurse. I hadn't read the note, but I knew what it said.

Lesson 7 The Writing Process: Personal Narrative

Write the revision of your first draft here or make changes to your computer document. As you revise, remember to keep readers interested by using descriptive words and active verbs.

_____

_____

_____

_____

_____

_____

_____

_____

_____

_____

_____

_____

_____

_____

_____

_____

_____

_____

_____

_____

_____

_____

_____

Now that you have revised your draft, are you still happy with your title? If not, write a new title here.

Title: _____

Lesson 7 The Writing Process: Personal Narrative

Proofread

Now is the time to correct those last errors. As you proofread, look for just one kind of error at a time. Read through once for capital letters, once for end punctuation, and once for spelling. Here is a checklist to help you proofread your revised narrative. Ask a friend to proofread your story and use the checklist, too.

> _____ Each sentence begins with a capital letter.
>
> _____ Each sentence ends with the correct punctuation (period, question mark, or exclamation point).
>
> _____ Each sentence states a complete thought.
>
> _____ All words are spelled correctly. (If you're not sure, check a dictionary.)

When proofreaders work, they use certain symbols. Using these symbols makes their job easier. They will make your job easier, too.

Use these symbols as you proofread your personal narrative. Also, read your writing out loud. Sometimes, you hear mistakes that you don't see.

> - $\underline{\underline{c}}$apitalize this letter.
> - Add a missing end mark: $_\odot$? !
> - Add a comma‸please.
> - Fix incorᵣect or misspelled words.
> - ~~Delete~~ this word.
> - Lowercase this Letter.

Publish

Write a final copy of your personal narrative on separate sheets of paper or make final changes to your computer document. Write or type carefully so that there are no mistakes.

You may wish to illustrate your story with drawings or photographs. Send your story as an e-mail attachment to a family member or friend.

Lesson 8 Parts of a Story

A good story has these ingredients:

- A story tells about made-up people or animals. They are the **characters** in the story.

- A story has a **setting** where the action takes place.

- A story's action is the **plot**. The plot is usually a series of events that includes a **conflict**, or problem, which needs to be solved.

- A story uses **dialogue**, or conversation among the characters, to move the action of the story along.

- An interesting **beginning**, **middle**, and **end** make a story fun to read.

- **Describing words** tell about the characters, setting, and events.

Read the first part of a science fiction story below. Then, answer the questions that follow.

The Colony

Even after 472 days, I hadn't gotten used to the quietness of this place. I was walking on hard ground, yet my footfalls hardly made a sound. In the distance, I could see the colony's generator. I knew it was churning and making noise, but I couldn't hear it at all. On Earth, I would have said that quietness was peaceful. Up here, though, the quiet just seemed empty.

An hour passed, and I was pleased at my progress. My distance meter showed that I was more than halfway. No one from the colony had walked as far as Monroe Flats before, and I wasn't exactly sure of what I would find along the way. I liked walking, but I hoped I wouldn't have to detour around any craters. I had plenty to do. As the colony's Environment Manager, I made daily tests on soil and atmosphere. They were vital to the colony's success.

With my head down, I worked my way up a slope when I saw something in the gray, dusty sand. I staggered backward, like a person who shies away from a snake. There was a track on the dusty hillside. I felt a sudden plunge in my stomach. *No one's been out here!* I thought. I looked to the left. The track continued about 40 meters, then wound around the curve of the slope. To the right, it went downward, to the base of the slope, and out of sight.

The track was just a sort of a swishy trail, as if someone had walked along dragging a heavy sack right behind, so that his or her footprints were covered. *Why would someone from the colony have been dragging something out here?* My mind was racing. *Surely I would have known.* Anyway, most people used transport modules when they were away from the colony. I kept looking left and right, as if I were checking for traffic. I jumped when my Telewave beeped.

"Morgan? Are you there?"

I spoke into the device on my wrist. "Yes, Chairman." The Chairman would know who else was out here.

Lesson 8 Parts of a Story

"Those supplies you ordered just arrived," the Chairman's voice said in its usual smooth tones.

"Oh," I waited, expecting more information. When it didn't come, I added, "Thank you, sir."

"Alright. See you tonight, Morgan."

"Yes, sir…Sir?" There was no response. The buzzing on my Telewave told me that there would be no further communication. Atmospheric disturbances often interrupted off-site transmissions.

I stood there feeling stupid because I couldn't decide what to do. I studied the track again to see if I could determine in which direction the person had been traveling. I noticed a pattern in the sand that seemed to indicate that the person had come from the bottom of the slope up to this point. I squinted up to the left. Nothing. Without really even deciding, I went in that direction.

Lesson 8 Parts of a Story

Answer these questions about "The Colony." Look back at the story on pages 37 and 38 if you need to.

Who is the main character in the story? _____

List three details about the main character.

_____ _____ _____

What other character appears in the story? _____

What do you know about this character?

_____

Where does the action take place?_____

What details does the writer reveal about the place? List some here.

_____ _____

_____ _____

What main problem occurs?_____

How does the main character deal with the problem at this point?

_____

Review the dialogue. Notice what the characters say and how they say it. What do you learn about the characters from the dialogue?

Main character:_____

_____

Other character: _____

_____

Record some of the story's sensory details. Remember to look for sights, sounds, smells, textures, and tastes.

_____ _____ _____

_____ _____ _____

_____ _____ _____

Lesson 9 Setting

Every story has to take place somewhere. The **setting** of a story is when and where the action takes place. The setting of a story may be in a real place or in a completely imagined place. The time during which a story takes place may be in the past, the present, or the future.

In some stories, readers learn details of the setting almost by accident. Perhaps a character complains about the "rotten weather," so you can assume it is cold or rainy. Maybe you learn from a character's thoughts that he is tired of sitting in the doctor's waiting room. In other stories, the narrator describes the setting. Here is an example from "A Mystery of Heroism," by Stephen Crane.

> Sometimes they of the infantry looked down at a fair little meadow which spread at their feet. Its long, green grass was rippling gently in a breeze. Beyond it was the grey form of a house half torn to pieces by shells and by the busy axes of soldiers who had pursued firewood. The line of an old fence was now dimly marked by long weeds and by an occasional post. A shell had blown the well-house to fragments. Little lines of grey smoke ribboning upward from some embers indicated the place where had stood the barn.

Look at all the information in that paragraph:

The characters—"they of the infantry"—are on a hill, because they "looked down" at the meadow. It is spring or summer; the grass is long and green. In contrast to the pleasant meadow are the remains of a battle. A house in the distance is standing in ruins, and a well-house and a barn are destroyed.

Now, think of a story or book that you have read. What do you remember about the setting? Remember to think about the time (such as the year), the weather, the time of day, and the physical location in all of its details. Write what you remember.

Title: _____

Setting: _____

_____

_____

_____

_____

_____

_____

_____

_____

Lesson 9 Setting

Here is another example. The setting is described by the main character, who is also the narrator. This passage is from "The Colony," the science fiction story you read on pages 37 and 38.

> Even after 472 days, I hadn't gotten used to the quietness of this place. I was walking on hard ground, yet my footfalls hardly made a sound. In the distance, I could see the colony's generator. I knew it was churning and making noise, but I couldn't hear it at all. On Earth, I would have said that quietness was peaceful. Up here, though, the quiet just seemed empty.

What information do you get about the setting from this passage?

_____

_____

_____

What mood, or feeling, do you get from the passage?

_____

What words or details convey that mood?

_____

Writers use details in their settings that match the mood of what is happening in the story. First, think about details that a writer might include in a story that is humorous or light-hearted.

What might the weather be like?

_____

What time of day might it be?

_____

Now, think about setting details that a writer might include in a scary part of a story, or in a part where something bad is going to happen to a character.

What might the weather be like?

_____

What time of day might it be?

_____

Look over the details you recorded for "light-hearted" settings and "scary" or "bad" settings. Are you starting to imagine a great story? Choose one of the settings you've already begun to visualize and develop it further on a separate sheet of paper.

Lesson 10 Characters

Some stories have terrific characters. Can you remember cheering for them when something good happened? Did you hope that the characters' bad times would turn out alright? Name some memorable characters you remember from stories or novels you have read.

_____   _____

_____   _____

Now, think about what you know about those characters. How did you learn about them? How did the narrator or author help you get to know the characters? Normally, readers learn about characters in four ways:

- The narrator reveals information.

- The characters' own words reveal information.

- The characters' actions reveal information.

- Other characters' words and actions reveal information.

Review "The Colony" on pages 37 and 38. What do you know about the main character? For each detail you record, write how you know it. For example, from the first sentence you learn that he has been somewhere for 472 days. You know this because the narrator (who is also the main character) reveals that information.

What I Know About the Character   **How I Know It**

_____   _____

_____   _____

_____   _____

_____   _____

_____   _____

_____   _____

_____   _____

_____   _____

_____   _____

_____   _____

_____   _____

Lesson 10 Characters

Now, think about a character you would like to create. Rather than thinking about what happens to the character, think about what kind of person the character is. Answer these questions.

Is the character human? _____ If not, what is the character? _____

Is the character male or female? _____

What two words best describe your character?

_____   _____

What does your character look like? Is he or she carrying something?

_____

What might your character say? How might your character say it? Write a line of dialogue that your character might speak.

_____

What might other characters say about this character? Either write some dialogue or describe what others would say.

_____

_____

_____

_____

Now, introduce your character. Write a paragraph about him or her.

_____

_____

_____

_____

_____

_____

_____

_____

_____

_____

_____

Lesson 11 Dialogue

Dialogue is the conversation among characters in a story. Good dialogue helps readers get to know the characters. It also keeps the action of the story moving. Here is what dialogue looks like.

> The Chairman looked thoughtfully out the window. "Morgan seemed a little distracted," he said. "I hope he's alright."
>
> Smiling, Kip replied, "Oh, I'm sure he is, sir."
>
> "How far did he say he was going?" asked the Chairman.
>
> Kip checked a chart. "To Monroe Flats, sir."
>
> "Monroe Flats!" burst the Chairman. "He's walking?"
>
> "Yes, sir," said Kip, a little surprised at the Chairman's outburst. "He likes to walk," Kip added, thinking it might calm his boss. It didn't.
>
> "Is he mad?" ranted the Chairman. "No one knows what's out there. Send a patrol in a transport module to get him. Right away."

What do you learn about the Chairman from this dialogue?

_____

What do you learn about Kip?

_____

Take a closer look at a line of dialogue and its punctuation.

Lesson 11 Dialogue

Below is some dialogue that has not been punctuated. Add the punctuation. Look at the dialogue on page 44 for examples if you need to. Pay close attention to the position of commas and end marks.

I wonder why the Chairman is so upset said Kip

The Chairman yelled Morgan should never have gone that far out

Is the transport module ready yet he asked

Dialogue should sound like real people talking. An 11-year-old character should sound more or less like you sound. An adult should sound like an adult. Remember, however, that people sound different from each other. People have different speech patterns based on where they grew up, what education they've had, and where they live.

Write a conversation between yourself and the Chairman, the leader of the space colony in the story on pages 37 and 38. Make the dialogue sound realistic. Stop and think how you would speak to a person who is in charge. How would he speak to you? Remember to use quotation marks and tag lines. Look at the examples on page 44 if you need to. The dialogue is started for you.

   "Sir, I received your Telewave message. Why did you ask me to bring a transport module?" I asked.

_____

_____

_____

_____

_____

_____

_____

_____

_____

_____

_____

_____

_____

_____

Lesson 12 Point of View

When a writer writes a story, he or she chooses a narrator to tell the story. In some stories, the narrator is one of the characters in the story. Words such as *I, me,* and *my* let readers know that this is happening. This is called **first-person point of view**. Here is another piece of "The Colony," the story begun on pages 37 and 38.

> As I followed the track, I realized that I was tight all over. My toes, fingers, and even my teeth were clenched. I jogged a few steps and shook my arms out. In training, they had always told you to stay relaxed. If you were tense, you couldn't respond as quickly. *Respond to what?* I thought. *Who in the world could be out here?*
>
> I suppose the jogging and unclenching distracted me. It wasn't until I was fully at the top of the hill that I saw the crater and what was in it. I automatically held my Telewave up to my mouth.
>
> "Jasper Colony, this is Morgan. Get me the Chairman," I said. A crackle assured me that my call was being transmitted. Then, the abrupt bark of the Chairman's voice made me jump.
>
> "Morgan, what are you doing out there?" the Chairman asked.

Here is the same scene, but it is written in **third-person point of view**. Readers see words such as *he, she, him, her, his, they,* and *them* in stories that are written in third person. The narrator is not a character in the story. The main character is the same, but the **omniscient**, or all-knowing, narrator "reports" to readers what the character says, thinks, and does.

> As he followed the track, Morgan realized that he was tight all over. His toes, fingers, and even his teeth were clenched. He jogged a few steps and shook his arms out. In training, they had always told him to stay relaxed. If he were tense, he couldn't respond as quickly. *Respond to what?* he thought. *Who in the world could be out here?*
>
> He supposed the jogging and the unclenching distracted him. It wasn't until he was fully at the top of the hill that he saw the crater and what was in it. He automatically held his Telewave up to his mouth.
>
> "Jasper Colony, this is Morgan. Get me the Chairman," he said. A crackle assured him that his call was being transmitted. Then, the abrupt bark of the Chairman's voice made him jump.
>
> "Morgan, what are you doing out there?" the Chairman asked. He felt that things were beginning to get out of hand.

Lesson 12 Point of View

Look back at the piece of the story on page 46. What do you think is in the crater? What happens next? Write the next paragraph in first-person point of view. Remember, in first person the narrator is a character in the story. Readers learn what he or she is thinking and feeling. The narrator does not know what other characters are thinking and feeling.

_____

_____

_____

_____

_____

_____

_____

_____

_____

_____

Now, write that same scene in third-person point of view. Remember, Morgan is still the main character. The all-knowing narrator is not a character, but will tell what Morgan says, thinks, and does. The narrator will also tell what any other character says, thinks, and does.

_____

_____

_____

_____

_____

_____

_____

_____

_____

_____

Lesson 13 Story Ideas

Many stories that you read are realistic. They include characters who are more or less normal. Realistic stories set in the past are called *historical fiction*. Whether the setting is in the past or the present, though, the characters could be real, and the events could happen, even though the details come from a writer's imagination.

List some stories or books you have read that have realistic settings. Briefly describe the settings.

Title   **Setting**

_____   _____

_____   _____

_____   _____

_____   _____

What kind of realistic story would you like to write? Will it be about an adventure that a kid had while he lived on the frontier in a log cabin? Will it be about a modern-day kid who is a computer genius? Realistic stories require just as much imagination as unrealistic, or fantasy, stories do. Write down some realistic story ideas.

Realistic story idea #1

Character(s):_____

Setting: _____

Plot: _____

_____

Realistic story idea #2

Character(s):_____

Setting: _____

Plot: _____

_____

Lesson 13 Story Ideas

Fiction that is set in the future is usually called *science fiction*. The setting may be on Earth or in another world of some sort. Characters may be human or some other life form. Details often involve advanced, or futuristic, technology that the author imagines.

What science fiction stories have you read? Try to recall some of the details. For example, were the characters human? Where did the characters live? Did the author reveal the year? Record a few details that you remember.

_____

_____

What kind of science fiction would you like to write? Who will be your main characters? Where will they live? Why are they there? What year is it? Open up your imagination and jot down a couple of science fiction ideas here.

Science fiction idea #1

Character(s):_____

Setting: _____

Plot: _____

_____

Science fiction idea #2

Character(s):_____

Setting: _____

Plot: _____

_____

Lesson 14 The Writing Process: Story

Some writers use their surroundings to help them create a character, setting, or plot for a story. Perhaps they base a character's home on a house they used to live in. Maybe a character's grandfather is much like the writer's grandfather. Other writers create whole new worlds. They imagine life in the future in ways that seem completely fantastic to readers. Use the writing process and see what kind of world you can create for a story.

Prewrite

Look at the story ideas you sketched out on pages 48 and 49. Choose one of those ideas or another idea that you like and begin to develop it. Whether you write a realistic story or science fiction, you need to pay special attention to your main character. Use this idea web to record details about how he or she looks, acts, speaks, and so on.

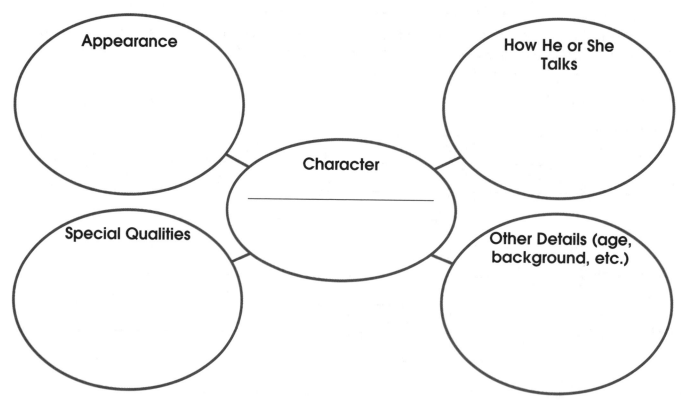

Before you continue, consider these questions about your setting and plot.

- What is the setting of your story? Consider place or location, time setting (year), season, time of day, weather, and so on.

- What problem will the character face?

- What does the character do to try to solve the problem? Does it take more than one try? What is the final solution or outcome?

Lesson 14 The Writing Process: Story

Now, put the main events of your story together. Think about the story you are about to tell. What is at the beginning, in the middle, and at the end? Use the story map on this page to plan the important parts of your story.

Character(s)
_____

Setting
_____

Plot: Beginning
_____
_____
_____
_____

Plot: Middle
_____
_____
_____
_____
_____
_____
_____

Plot: End
_____
_____
_____
_____

Lesson 14 The Writing Process: Story

Draft

Write a first draft of your story here or in a computer document. Refer to your story map as you write. Don't forget to include dialogue and transition words to move the action along. Continue on another sheet of paper if you need to. As you write, don't worry about mistakes. Just get your ideas down in sentences and in order.

_____

_____

_____

_____

_____

_____

_____

_____

_____

_____

_____

_____

_____

_____

_____

_____

_____

_____

_____

_____

_____

_____

Write some ideas for a title here. You may choose the final title later.

Title: _____

Lesson 14 The Writing Process: Story

Revise

Every writer must look at his or her work with fresh eyes and figure out how to make the writing better. Even experienced writers do this, and no one considers it an easy job.

Answer the questions below. If you answer "no" to any of these questions, those are the areas you might need to improve. Make marks on your draft so you know what needs attention. Ask a friend to read your draft and answer the questions, too.

> - Did you give details about an interesting character and a setting?
> - Does your story have a beginning, a middle, and an end?
> - Did you include a problem and a solution in your plot?
> - Did you tell events in an order that made sense?
> - Did you use sensory details?
> - Did you use dialogue to help readers learn about characters and to move the story forward?
> - Did you use transition and time-order words?
> - Did you write a good conclusion?
> - Did you use either first person or third person narration throughout the story?

Review the important parts of a story.

- In the **beginning** of a story, readers meet the character or characters and learn a little about the setting and the plot. The first sentence makes readers want to keep on reading.
- In the **middle** of a story, the action takes place. Readers see the character or characters face a problem. The characters probably make one or more attempts to solve the problem.
- In the **end**, the characters solve the problem in a logical way. Keep in mind that it is not satisfying to have a story's central problem just go away by magic or by coincidence. Your characters must deal with or solve their problem.

On your draft, draw brackets next to the beginning, middle, and end of your story. Jot some notes if you decide that you must revise any of those parts to make them more interesting for your readers.

Lesson 14 The Writing Process: Story

Read your draft out loud. Listen for awkward sentences or sentences that sound too much the same. Then, write the revision of your story here or make changes to your computer document. Fix those awkward sentences as you go.

_____

_____

_____

_____

_____

_____

_____

_____

_____

_____

_____

_____

_____

_____

_____

_____

_____

_____

_____

_____

_____

_____

_____

Review your title choices. Which one seems best? Write it here.

Title: _____

Lesson 14 The Writing Process: Story

Proofread

By now, you have read your story several times. You can probably recite parts from memory. It is still important, though, to proofread carefully. When you are familiar with what you are reading, you are more likely to overlook errors. Also, you must still proofread typewritten text, even if the computer has checked your spelling. If you type *form* instead of *from*, for example, the computer won't catch that error. Use the checklist below as you proofread your revised story. Read for one kind of error at a time. Ask a friend to proofread your story and use the checklist, too.

_____ Each sentence begins with a capital letter.

_____ Each sentence ends with the correct punctuation (period, question mark, or exclamation point).

_____ Dialogue is punctuated correctly.

_____ Each sentence states a complete thought.

_____ All words are spelled correctly.

When proofreaders work, they use certain symbols. Using these symbols will make your job easier.

Use these symbols as you proofread your story. Remember to read your writing out loud to yourself. When you read out loud, you may hear mistakes or rough spots that you did not see.

- C̲apitalize this letter.
- Add a missing end mark: ⊙ ? !
- Add a comma‸please.
- "Be sure to punctuate your dialogue,"she said.
- Fix incorᵉct or misspelled words.
- ~~Delete~~ this word.
- Lowercase this ʟetter.

Publish

Write a final copy of your story on separate sheets of paper or make final changes to your computer document. Write or type carefully so there are no mistakes. If you wish, add illustrations and make a title page. With an adult's permission, post your story on a good Web site that publishes young people's writing (do not include your name).

You read explanatory writing every day. Explanatory writing usually comes in the form of instructions. Some explanations are simple. A sign says "Use Other Door" and you know what to do. Some explanations are not simple. A new board game might come with a whole book full of instructions. A piece of furniture might come in a small box with instructions that help you assemble the parts.

Some explanations are not instructions, though. Some explanations tell how or why something happened. For example, your teacher might explain what events cause an earthquake. You might read an explanation of why people migrate from one continent to another.

List some explanations that you have read or heard this week.

_____   _____

_____   _____

Think about instructions you have read or used. How many different kinds can you list?

_____ _____ _____

_____ _____ _____

When you write to explain, or give instructions, you might write for these reasons:

- to tell how to make something
- to tell how something works
- to tell how to get somewhere
- to tell why something happened

Lesson 1 Explanatory Writing

Here is a simple explanation that tells how to make Judy's idea of the perfect piece of toast.

First, I toast a piece of whole wheat bread. I set the toaster on setting #1 because I like my bread lightly toasted. As soon as the toast pops up, I spread butter on it. This is important because the butter needs to melt. Then, I sprinkle cinnamon and sugar from the shaker onto the toast, right to the edges. It soaks into the melted butter and makes a delicious part of my breakfast.

The writer stated each step in order. To help readers follow the steps, she used order words such as *first, as soon as,* and *then* to make the order very clear. Underline each of those order words that you find in the paragraph.

What do you know how to do? Write down a few simple processes, such as making toast, that you can explain clearly.

_____   _____

_____   _____

Now, choose one of the processes you listed and think carefully about each of its steps. Imagine that you are explaining the process to someone who has never done it before. You'll have to start at the very beginning. List the steps here.

Process: _____

Step 1: _____

Step 2: _____

Step 3: _____

Step 4: _____

Step 5: _____

Step 6: _____

Step 7: _____

Step 8: _____

Step 9: _____

Step 10: _____

Step 11: _____

Step 12: _____

Lesson 2 Directions

A new student teacher stops you in the hall and asks for directions to the cafeteria. Can you give clear directions to help him or her find the way?

Directions need to be in order. As you write them, think about what happens first, second, next, and so on. In addition, directions need to tell where. Here are some words that are often used in directions.

Direction Words	Position Words	Order Words
left	over	first
right	under	second
up	past	then
down	beyond	next
north	before	after that
west	above	finally
	beside	

Mikayla told the new student teacher how to get to the cafeteria. Underline the direction, position, and order words in the paragraph.

First, go down the big stairway at the end of the hall. At the bottom of the stairs, go straight. Go past the main entrance. Then, turn right and go down the blue hallway. At the end of that hall, look left, and you'll see the cafeteria beyond the big glass doors.

Lesson 2 Directions

Write directions that tell how to get from your classroom to the cafeteria. If you need to, close your eyes and imagine walking from here to there. Now, write your directions. If you need to, look back to page 58 for direction, position, and order words to use.

_____

_____

_____

_____

_____

_____

_____

_____

You have decided to invite friends to visit you in your remote mountain cabin. They will have to hike up the mountain from the nearest village. Write directions so they can find the way. If you wish, make a sketch of this make-believe path. Then, write the directions here.

_____

_____

_____

_____

_____

_____

_____

_____

_____

_____

Lesson 3 The Writing Process: How-to Instructions

You may be called upon at any time to explain how to do something. Maybe a friend wants to know how to finish level 19 of your favorite computer game. Perhaps someone asks you to explain the rules of wrestling. Use the writing process to see how good you are at explaining to someone else how to do something.

Prewrite

Think about things that you know how to do. You might know how to make a great after-school snack, or maybe you can shape balloons into amazing animals. Write down some things that you know how to do.

_____   _____

_____   _____

_____   _____

Look over your list and imagine explaining how to do each thing. With which topic are you most comfortable? Explore the idea by writing down everything you can think of about that topic.

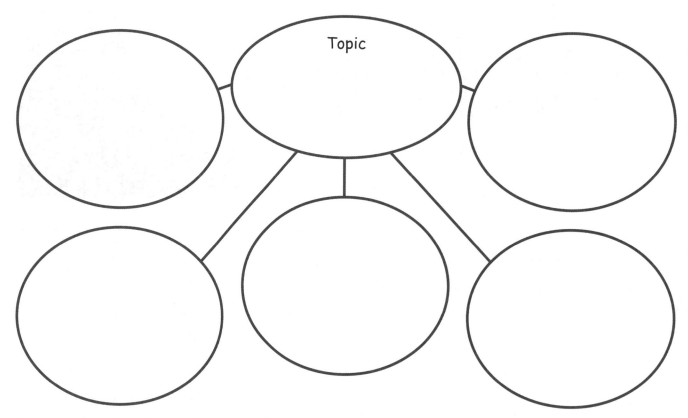

Are you comfortable with your topic? If not, go back to your list and choose another. Explore it with an idea web on a separate sheet of paper. Remember to think about your audience. What will they need to know?

Lesson 3 The Writing Process: How-to Instructions

Now, it is time to put the steps in order. Think about the process you are about to explain. Assume that your audience has never done this before, so you need to start at the very beginning. Use the sequence chart on this page to list the important steps in your explanation. Don't worry about details here; just be sure to list the main steps in the correct order.

1. _____

↓

2. _____

↓

3. _____

↓

4. _____

↓

5. _____

↓

6. _____

↓

7. _____

↓

8 _____

↓

9. _____

Lesson 3 The Writing Process: How-to Instructions

Draft

Write a first draft of your instructions in the space below or in a computer document. Keep your sequence chart handy as you write. Use time-order words to help your reader understand. Continue on another sheet of paper if you need to. Don't worry about getting everything perfect. Just get your ideas down in sentences and in order.

_____

_____

_____

_____

_____

_____

_____

_____

_____

_____

_____

_____

_____

_____

_____

_____

_____

_____

_____

_____

_____

_____

_____

_____

Lesson 3 The Writing Process: How-to Instructions

Revise

For many writers, revising is much more difficult than writing the first draft. Reread your work with fresh eyes. Answer the questions below about your draft. If you answer "no" to any of these questions, those areas might need improvement. Make marks on your draft so you know what needs more work. Ask a friend to read your draft and answer the questions, too.

- Did you explain how to do something from beginning to end?
- Did you include all of the steps in order?
- Did you include time-order words to make the sequence clear?
- Did you use direction and position words to make your details clear?
- Did you use good describing words so your readers can "see" what they are supposed to do?
- Did you keep your audience in mind by asking yourself what they might already know or what they need to know?
- Did you include a heading or title so readers know what they are reading about?
- Did you include a concluding statement so readers know what happens at the end?

Recognizing causes and effects helps readers understand what they are reading. The words *so*, *because*, *therefore*, and *as a result* may signal a cause-effect relationship. Here is an example:

Slam the clay against the tabletop. This removes air bubbles from the clay. Continue working the clay so that it becomes soft. Do not fold the clay or poke your fingers into it because that would result in new air bubbles.

Look back at your draft and think about cause-and-effect relationships. Are the causes and effects clear? Do you need to add signal words to make them more clear? Can you add a visual aid to help the reader understand better?

Lesson 3 The Writing Process: How-to Instructions

Write the revision of your first draft here or make changes to your computer document. As you revise, remember to think about important details that your readers will need to know.

_____

_____

_____

_____

_____

_____

_____

_____

_____

_____

_____

_____

_____

_____

_____

_____

_____

_____

_____

_____

_____

_____

_____

_____

_____

_____

_____

_____

Lesson 3 The Writing Process: How-to Instructions

Proofread

Now is the time to correct any last little mistakes. You will be a better proofreader if you look for just one kind of error at a time. Read through once for capital letters. Read again for end punctuation, spelling, and so on. Here is a checklist to use as you proofread your instructions. Ask a friend to proofread your writing and use the checklist, too.

_____ Each sentence begins with a capital letter.

_____ Each sentence ends with the correct punctuation (period, question mark, or exclamation point).

_____ Each sentence states a complete thought.

_____ All words are spelled correctly. (If you're not sure, check a dictionary.)

Use standard proofreading symbols as you proofread your own revised instructions.

As you proofread, remember to read your writing out loud, even if there is no one to listen. When you read, you may hear mistakes or awkward spots that you did not see.

- capitalize this letter.
- Add a missing end mark: ⊙ ? !
- Insert a comma please.
- Fix incorect or misspelled words.
- Delete this word.
- Lowercase this Letter.

Publish

Write a final copy of your instructions on separate sheets of paper or make final changes to your computer document. Write or type carefully so there are no mistakes. If you wish, include a graph, chart, or diagram to enhance your instructions and make them clearer. Read your instructions out loud or perform a demonstration in front of an audience.

Lesson 4 Cause-and-Effect Relationships

Why are school buses yellow? Why is cheese orange? When you ask why, you are looking for causes. A **cause** is a reason why something happens. An **effect** is a thing that happens. Here are some examples of causes and effects. Think about the relationship between each cause and effect.

Cause	Effect
It is raining.	Track practice is held indoors.
The lawn mower is broken.	The grass is knee high.
Tamara broke a tooth.	She went to the dentist today.

When writers write to inform, they often use causes and effects. They use the words and phrases *so, because, as a result,* and *therefore* to link causes and effects. Read this paragraph about why earthquakes occur. Circle the cause-and-effect words and phrases in the paragraph.

The surface of Earth consists of huge geologic plates. On these plates rest the oceans and continents. The place where two plates meet is called a *fault*. Sometimes, one plate or the other shifts, so they rub against each other at the fault line. If there is enough shifting, something has to give. Both plates may buckle, or one plate may slip up over the edge of the other. Whatever the type of movement, if it is significant, the surface of Earth shakes or heaves as a result.

Can you find some causes and effects in that paragraph? One is written for you. Write two other causes and effects.

Cause	Effect
Earth's plates shift.	The plates rub against each other.

Lesson 4 Cause-and-Effect Relationships

Writers might also use causes and effects when they tell about events that happened in a story or novel. The paragraph below explains some causes and effects from *Hatchet* by Gary Paulsen.

The pilot suffers a heart attack during the flight. As a result, Brian must land the plane. Though he does so successfully, he is hurt and alone in the wilderness. Brian must protect himself, so he builds a shelter and makes spears. He must eat, so he learns to spear fish. Because Brian uses his wits, he manages to survive.

Find the causes and effects in the paragraph above. Write them here. The first one is done for you.

Cause	Effect
The pilot suffers a heart attack.	Brian must land the plane.

Think about a story or novel you have read recently. What happened, and what did the characters do? Think about the events in terms of causes and effects. Ask yourself questions such as these: What caused this event to happen? What effect did this event have?

Write the causes and effects of some important events from the book.

Title: _____

Cause	Effect

Lesson 5 Report an Event

In a news report, a reporter writes about an event. The event might be a political convention, a traffic accident, or a warehouse explosion. In addition to relating events in the order in which they occurred, the reporter links causes and effects. Causes and effects help readers understand what happens and why.

Here is part of a report about a traffic accident. Look for words that signal cause-and-effect relationships: *so, because, as a result, therefore.* When you find them, circle them.

Car Crash on I-23

The vehicle, driven by Lincoln Marsh, age 37, went out of control because of an oil slick on the road surface. As a result, Marsh's vehicle left the roadway. Because the guardrail is being replaced, the temporary railing that was in place failed to stop the vehicle. The vehicle went down an embankment and lodged in the branches of a large tree. Mr. Marsh suffered only minor injuries. Since the temporary railing did not work, an investigation will be performed.

Write two causes and two effects from the paragraph.

Cause:_____   Effect: _____

_____   _____

_____   _____

Cause:_____   Effect: _____

_____   _____

_____   _____

Lesson 5 Report an Event

Now, think about causes and effects for an event in your own life. What happened yesterday? Even if nothing exciting happened, there were causes and effects in action. What did you do? What happened next? What resulted from these happenings? List some events in order. Draw arrows to show any cause-and-effect relationship among events.

1. _____

2. _____

3. _____

4. _____

5. _____

Now, practice writing about causes and effects. Write a paragraph about the happenings you listed above. Remember to use *so, because, as a result, therefore,* and other signal words to connect the cause-and-effect relationships.

_____

_____

_____

_____

_____

_____

_____

_____

_____

_____

_____

_____

_____

_____

_____

_____

_____

_____

_____

_____

Lesson 6 Spatial Organization

When you walk into a room, you probably look around in an organized way. You might scan the room from left to right or from right to left. How you look at a room might depend on the size or shape of the room, what is in the room, or what is happening in the room.

When writers give information about a room or some other place, they describe it in an organized way. This organization helps readers "see" the place just as if they were looking at it themselves. In the description of a skyscraper below, a writer describes the huge building from bottom to top.

> Just walking past on the sidewalk, you would never suspect anything. The doors were normal revolving glass doors. Through other windows, you could see people walking about in the lobby. But above the sidewalk, the building just kept going and going. Rows of windows blurred into one another. Beyond them, antennas and cell towers stretched even higher.

When organizing ideas by space, use words that tell where things are. Here are some common spatial words. Circle these, or other spatial words, in the paragraph above.

above	across	beside	between	beyond	into	left
low	middle	next to	over	right	through	under

Now, look at the room around you. Practice noticing details in an organized way. Write down what you see in the room. Use spatial words to describe where things are.

Left: _____

_____

Straight ahead: _____

_____

Right: _____

_____

Lesson 6 Spatial Organization

Imagine that you have climbed a mountain. At last, you are standing on the summit. What do you see? Describe the most distant detail first. Then, go on to describe what is in the middle distance, then what is nearest to you. Use sensory details so that readers can see, hear, smell, and feel the view. Also, remember to use spatial words to tell where things are.

_____

_____

_____

_____

_____

_____

_____

_____

_____

Imagine you are a member of a mountain climbing group. In your journal, you want to record the whole experience, so you describe the gear everyone is wearing. Organize the details of your description from top to bottom or from bottom to top.

_____

_____

_____

_____

_____

_____

_____

_____

_____

Lesson 7 The Language of Comparison

To compare two things, use the ending **-er** or the word *more* to talk and write about how the two things are different. These are **comparative** words and phrases.

> The first bear is *larger than* the second bear.

> The first bear is also *more monstrous than* the second bear.

For short words, such as *large*, add the **-er** ending. For longer words, such as *monstrous*, use *more* to compare.

Do some more comparing.

> Your snake is *fatter than* mine.

> My snake is *skinnier than* yours.

For some words, such as *red*, double the final consonant, then add the **-er** ending. For words that end in **y**, change the **y** to **i**, then add **er**.

Note: *More* and the **-er** ending are never used at the same time. For example, it is not correct to write, "I ran more faster than you did."

Look at the pictures and compare them. Use comparative forms of the words given to complete each sentence below.

> One bed is _____ than the other. (lumpy)

> That bed must be _____ than the other. (uncomfortable)

> I would rather sleep on the _____ bed. (neat)

Write your own sentence about the beds. Use a comparative word or phrase. Remember to follow the spelling hints when you use **er** to end your comparing word.

_____

_____

Lesson 7 The Language of Comparison

When talking or writing about how three or more things are different, use the ending **-est** or the word *most*. These are **superlative** words and phrases.

The elephant is the *heaviest* of the three animals.

The dog has the *longest* fur.

The mouse has the *most delicate* feet.

The same spelling changes that occur when you add **er** to a word occur when you add **est** to a word. For example, *happiest* and *maddest* are correct spellings of superlative words.

Take your turn comparing three objects. Look at the pictures. Then, use the words *slow*, *speedy*, and *graceful* in sentences that compare the animals.

_____

_____

_____

_____

_____

_____

Errors in comparative and superlative words and phrases are common. Remember, use the ending **-er** or *more* when comparing two things. Use the ending **-est** or *most* when comparing three or more things. Can you find the errors in these comparisons? Write the correct comparative or superlative word or phrase on the line after each sentence.

Of my two dogs, Rex is the smartest. _____

Taylor is the taller of all the boys in the class. _____

That surprise birthday party was my most happiest moment. _____

Tara is the oldest of my two sisters. _____

Lesson 8 Comparing Characters

When you read, it is only natural to compare a book you are reading with other books you have read. You may note how situations or characters are alike or different. Comparing characters, whether within a book or among different books, can actually help you understand a story and its developments.

You already know how to compare things with the help of a Venn diagram. Emily made a diagram in her reader response journal to record what she knows so far about two characters in a book her class is reading.

<u>Countdown</u> by Ben Mikaelsen

Elliot — Both Characters — Vincent

in Montana

chosen as teenage astronaut

lives on ranch

dreamers

in conflict with fathers

in Kenya

Maasai

learns white men's ways from Sambeke

Think of characters in a book you are reading or have read lately. How are they alike and different? Fill out this Venn diagram with what you know about the characters. Think about how the characters act, or how they respond to what happens to them. Remember to label the circles with the characters' names.

_____

_____ Both Characters _____

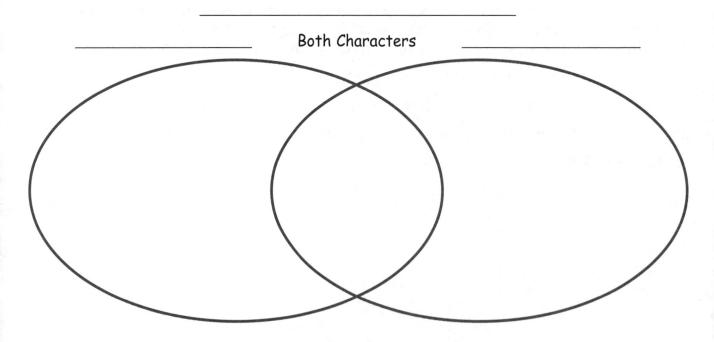

Lesson 8 Comparing Characters

There are two common ways to organize a written comparison. One way is to write first about one thing, then about the other. This is a **whole-to-whole comparison**. Read the example below. Information about the character Elliot is in red. Information about the character Vincent is in blue.

> Elliot is a 14-year-old with a lot of responsibility. His dad depends on him to help take care of cattle on the family's ranch. He longs to go to space, and NASA has accepted him as a teenage astronaut. However, Elliot's father doesn't understand Elliot's dream and doesn't want him to leave home. Vincent is also 14 years old and also takes care of cattle. His family are Maasai herders in Kenya. Vincent takes the cattle out to graze and protects them from danger. Vincent has a friend, Sambeke, who teaches him new ideas about white people. Vincent's father does not approve and does not want Vincent to spend time with Sambeke.

The other way to compare is to write first about one feature, or characteristic, as it relates to both objects. Then, go on to another feature, and so on. This is a **part-to-part comparison**. Here is an example. Again, information about Elliot is in red; information about Vincent is in blue.

> Elliot is a 14-year old who lives on a ranch in Montana. He has a great deal of responsibility helping his father with the cattle. Vincent is also 14 years old, but he lives on the other side of the world in Kenya with the Maasai people. Like Elliot, he is responsible for taking care of cattle and keeping them safe. Elliot longs to be an astronaut. To his delight, he is chosen to be a teenage astronaut. This causes a big argument with his father. Elliot's dad does not want him to leave the ranch and go to space. Although Vincent also experiences conflict with his father, it revolves around Vincent's friendship with Sambeke, a boy who teaches him new ideas about white people. Vincent's father does not approve of the friendship. Just like Elliot's father, Vincent's father wants him to stay home and help with cattle herding.

Now, review your own Venn diagram on page 74. On another sheet of paper, write a comparison of the two characters you chose. Decide whether you will use whole-to-whole or part-to-part organization.

Lesson 9 The Writing Process: Comparing Literature

You have read many books from different genres such as fantasy, science fiction, historical fiction, and nonfiction. All types of literature have some things in common: characters, settings, events, and themes. It can be very interesting to think about what is the same and what is different about two books you have read. Writing a comparison between two books or stories can help you see each one in a new way.

Prewrite

The books *Heroes of the Environment* by Harriet Rohmer is nonfiction. *California Blue,* by David Klass, is a realistic fiction story. The books are different, but they both have the theme of people trying to help the environment. Look at the Venn diagram comparing the two books.

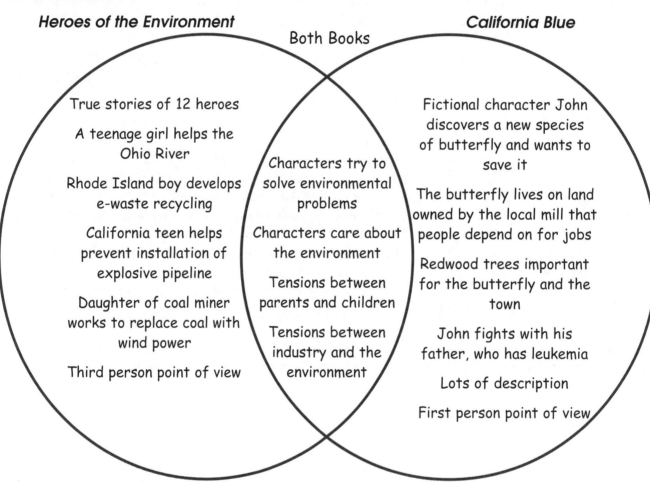

Heroes of the Environment   Both Books   *California Blue*

True stories of 12 heroes

A teenage girl helps the Ohio River

Rhode Island boy develops e-waste recycling

California teen helps prevent installation of explosive pipeline

Daughter of coal miner works to replace coal with wind power

Third person point of view

Characters try to solve environmental problems

Characters care about the environment

Tensions between parents and children

Tensions between industry and the environment

Fictional character John discovers a new species of butterfly and wants to save it

The butterfly lives on land owned by the local mill that people depend on for jobs

Redwood trees important for the butterfly and the town

John fights with his father, who has leukemia

Lots of description

First person point of view

The two books compared above have many differences. They are from different genres and are shelved in two completely different sections of the library. However, they have many similarities, too. Both books are about people who try to help the environment and the problems they encounter while trying to reach their goals.

Lesson 9 The Writing Process: Comparing Literature

Think of books you have read and enjoyed from different genres. They may be fantasy, historical fiction, nonfiction, realistic fiction, mystery, or biography. Write their titles on the lines below.

_____   _____

_____   _____

_____   _____

Now, select two books from different genres that have a similar theme or topic. For example, you would not choose to compare *The Red Kimono* by Jan Morrill (about a girl and her brother in a Japanese internment camp during World War II) with *Bunnicula* by Deborah and James Howe (about a vampire rabbit and a dog). These books are about different topics, and they have few similarities. However, you could compare *Helen Keller: The Story of My Life* by Helen Keller (autobiography of a woman born unable to see or hear) with *Anything But Typical* by Nora Raleigh Baskin (realistic fiction about a boy with autism who loves to write stories). These books are different, but they are both about people who struggle to overcome disabilities.

Draw stars above beside the titles of two books that you will compare. Make sure they are from different genres. Write them above the circles below and fill in the Venn diagram to compare the two stories.

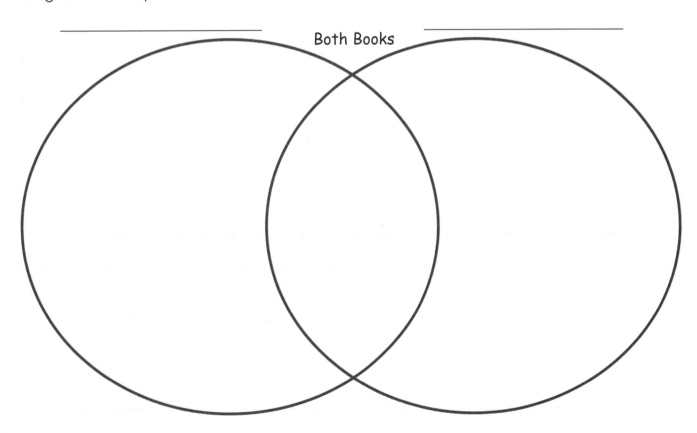

Both Books

Lesson 9 The Writing Process: Comparing Literature

Now, it is time to organize the points you will make in your comparison. Decide whether you will write a whole-to-whole comparison or a part-to-part comparison (see page 75). No matter which strategy you choose, your comparison should include a beginning (or introduction), a middle (or body), and an ending (or conclusion). The introduction should include the titles and authors of both books. The body should compare the two works of literature in detail. The conclusion should focus on the theme shared by both books and explain why it is important.

Below, write ideas for each section of your comparison.

Introduction

Body

Conclusion

Lesson 9 The Writing Process: Comparing Literature

Draft

Write a first draft of your comparison on this page or in a computer document. As you write, refer to your chart on page 78. Continue on another sheet of paper if you need to. Remember to use comparison words and transition words. Include a good ending, or conclusion. For now, don't worry about mistakes. Just get your ideas down in order.

_____

_____

_____

_____

_____

_____

_____

_____

_____

_____

_____

_____

_____

_____

_____

_____

_____

_____

_____

_____

_____

_____

_____

Now that you have completed your draft, write an idea for a title here.

Title: _____

Lesson 9 The Writing Process: Comparing Literature

Revise

Even the most experienced writers read over their work and make changes. If possible, set your writing aside for a few hours. Then, reread your comparison slowly and carefully. Answer the questions below about your draft. If you answer "no" to any of these questions, those areas might need improvement. Feel free to make marks on your draft, so you know what needs more work. Ask a friend to read your draft and answer the questions, too.

- Did you introduce the two books you are comparing?
- Did you explain how the books are similar and different?
- Did you use whole-to-whole or part-to-part organization?
- Did you use comparison words?
- Did you link your ideas using transition words?
- Did you explain why the topic or theme in both books is important?
- Did you write a good conclusion?

Review these transition words and phrases. They may help you to compare and contrast the two books when you revise your writing.

yet	however	as well as
but	similarly	on one hand
still	instead of	on the other hand
likewise	in contrast	on the contrary
rather	especially	for this reason

Rewrite your comparison on separate sheets of paper or make changes to your computer document. As you revise, remember to organize your points well, use transition words, and include a good ending.

Lesson 9 The Writing Process: Comparing Literature

Proofread

By now, you have read your comparison several times. You can probably recite parts from memory. It is still important, though, to proofread carefully. When you are familiar with what you are reading, you are more likely to overlook errors. Also, you must still proofread typewritten text, even if the computer has checked your spelling. If you type *form* instead of *from*, for example, the computer won't catch that error. Use the checklist below as you proofread your revised story. Read for one kind of error at a time. Ask a friend to read your writing and use the checklist, too.

_____ Each sentence begins with a capital letter.

_____ Each sentence ends with the correct punctuation (period, question mark, or exclamation point).

_____ Each sentence states a complete thought.

_____ All words are spelled correctly.

When proofreaders work, they use certain symbols. Using these symbols will make your job easier.

Use these symbols as you proofread your comparison. Remember to read your writing out loud to yourself. When you read out loud, you may hear mistakes or rough spots that you did not see.

- c̠ capitalize this letter.
- Add a missing end mark: ⊙ ? !
- Add a comma‸please.
- Fix incorᵣect or misspelled words.
- D̶e̶l̶e̶t̶e̶ this word.
- Lowercase this ℓetter.

Publish

Write a final copy of your comparison on separate sheets of paper or make final changes to your computer document. Write or type carefully so there are no mistakes. Share your writing with others. You may wish to ask your school librarian to display your essay.

Lesson 10 Informational Writing

When your teachers assign a report, they are asking you to inform them about what you know or have learned. When you write to inform, you present information about a topic. Here is a report that Ashley wrote about linen.

Linen

Three centuries ago, clothing made of linen was fairly common. Hard-working colonists in North America wore it at work and play. Today, linen fabric is likely to be made into sporty or dressy clothing, but never work clothing.

Linen fabric was familiar to the early Americans because it was in use throughout Europe. Once they migrated to North America, it was costly to import fabric, so the colonists learned to make their own. To do so, they had to raise a crop of flax.

To make linen, a farmer first harvests the flax plants. He wants the fibers to be as long as possible, so he pulls the plants rather than cut them. The stems are then soaked in water for as long as three weeks. This loosens the inner fibers. Then, the flax is dried and passed through rollers to separate the useful inner fiber from the tough part of the stem. Next, the stems are beaten to free the fibers from the unwanted parts. Finally, the fibers are hackled, or combed, to clean and straighten the desirable fibers. After hackling, the fiber is ready to be spun into thread, then woven into fabric.

The type of linen fabric that results depends on the quality of the fibers and the care taken during processing. If the fiber is coarse, it may be made into rope, canvas, or carpet backing. If the fiber is fine, it may be woven into fabric for fine clothing, or it may become the most delicate of handkerchiefs. The role of linen has changed, but it is still an important fabric that contributes to our daily lives.

Notice how Ashley uses formal language. She does not write the report as if she were talking to a friend. She avoids using contractions such as *don't, won't, can't,* and *hasn't.* She writes from a third-person point of view, and so does not use the word *I.* She reports facts carefully and accurately.

Lesson 10 Informational Writing

When writers write to inform, they use transition words to connect ideas. **Transition words** help readers understand connections among ideas. Here are some common transition words:

again	before long	in addition
also	but	in spite of
and	consequently	therefore
as a result	finally	thus
at the same time	for example	when
because	however	

Look back at Ashley's report on page 82. Find the transition words that she used. Circle them.

Now, explore what you could write a report about. It is always a good idea to choose a topic in which you are interested. If you are studying world history and you think pyramids are boring, don't choose pyramids for your topic. Instead, choose to write about Greek myths or the products that were traded on the Silk Road. To help you think of possible topics, answer these questions.

What are some places in the world that interest you or that you would like to visit?

_____ _____ _____

_____ _____ _____

What are some historical places or events that you know about? It might be an ancient city, a battleground, or a historical person's home.

_____ _____

_____ _____

Here are the features of informational writing:

- It gives important information about a topic.
- It presents a main idea, which is supported with facts.
- It may include information from several different sources.
- It draws a conclusion based on the information presented.
- It is organized in a logical way. Transition words connect ideas.

Lesson 11 Reliable Sources

Information is everywhere around you. You can get information from a book, from a Web site, and even from a cell phone. Which sources of information are best? How can you tell which are good and which are not good?

First, think about the kinds of sources available. For each question, write the source that would be most useful based on the type of information required. For some questions, more than one source might be useful.

dictionary newspaper atlas	print encyclopedia online encyclopedia	almanac Web site

_____ What is the world record for the high jump?

_____ How many acres of rain forest exist today?

_____ When did the Crusades occur?

_____ Where is the Yangtze River?

_____ What did the school board discuss at its monthly meeting?

_____ What does *jargon* mean?

_____ What kinds of ancient historical artifacts have been found on the island of Crete?

Lesson 11 Reliable Sources

Once you find a source that seems to have the information you need, you must decide whether the source is reliable. If the source is printed, ask yourself these questions:

- **When was this source published?** If you need current information, the source should be only one or two years old. Depending on the subject, even that might be too old.

- **Who wrote this source and for what purpose?** If the source is an encyclopedia, atlas, or almanac, you can be pretty confident that responsible authors wrote it to provide information. If it is a magazine article or a work of nonfiction, you need to ask more questions. Might there be bias in the material (see page 109)? Read the book jacket or an "About the Author" blurb to discover as much as you can about the expertise of the author and the purpose for writing.

If you are looking at an online source, there are some other questions to ask. Keep in mind that anyone can create a Web site. Just because you see information on a Web site does not mean that it is accurate.

- **What person or organization established or maintains this Web site? What is the purpose of the site?** What makes this person or organization an expert on the topic?

- **What is the purpose of the site?** Whether a person or an organization maintains a site, there is the potential for bias. Does the person or organization want to inform, to sell something, or to present a certain point of view (which may or may not be biased)?

- **When was the site last updated?** Just as with print sources, the publication date may matter, depending on whether you need current information.

Write *yes* or *no* to indicate whether these sources would be reliable.

_____ You are writing about a recent natural disaster. You consult a report on the National Weather Service's Web site.

_____ You are writing about Egypt's pyramids and how they were built. You refer to an article in a history magazine that was published 18 years ago.

_____ You are writing an article about testing in schools. You go to your state's Department of Education Web site to collect data.

_____ You are writing an article on skateboard safety. You cite www.Kensboards. com, which is a site that sells custom-make skateboards.

A good report draws on several different sources. For example, if you are writing about a recent natural disaster, look at newspaper articles, disaster-relief Web sites, encyclopedia articles about the area, and published interviews with witnesses.

Lesson 12 Summaries, Quotes, and Paraphrases

As you research, you will read many books, articles, and Web sites. You will collect lots of information. However, there will not be room in your report to include all the facts you gather. You must choose only the most important information that helps to explain your topic. You must also be careful to put ideas from your sources into your own words. If you copy an author's words and present them as your own, you are committing **plagiarism**. Taking credit for another writer's words or ideas is a form of cheating.

Your research notes may take the form of summaries, quotes, or paraphrases. For his report, Aaron read this passage from the book *Marvelous Machines* by T. Pinch.

> The first bicycle to really make an impact was the safety bicycle. It rode low to the ground. The major problem with the safety bicycle was that it did not have tires, which made riding it on cobblestone streets a rather jarring experience. As a result of consumer feedback, bicycle manufacturers developed rubber tires, which helped to make the bike riding experience much more smooth and comfortable.

A **summary** states the main ideas, in the writer's own words, in a few sentences. Aaron wrote this summary.

> It took a while for the modern bicycle to develop. One of the first bicycles, the safety bicycle, had no tires! Its bumpy ride led manufacturers to invent rubber bike tires.

A **quote** is an exact copy of words from the source. If these words are included in the final report, they must be enclosed in quotation marks and preceded by the original author's name. Aaron wrote this quote.

> According to Pinch, the invention of the tire "helped to make the bike riding experience much more smooth and comfortable."

A **paraphrase** restates facts or ideas in the writer's own words. If the information is the author's own idea (and not a widely known fact), you need to give the author credit. However, you do not need to use quotation marks. Aaron wrote the paraphrase below. Notice how he says almost the same thing as the author. However, he uses his own words to say it.

> Pinch explains that, with the invention of the rubber tire, bike riding became a more pleasant experience.

Lesson 12 Summaries, Quotes, and Paraphrases

Pretend you are writing a report on how lollipops are made. Read the passage below from *A History of Hard Candy* by Alisa Conrad.

Lollipops are relatively easy to make. Almost all lollipops have only four ingredients: sugar, water, flavoring, and food coloring. Lollipop manufacturers combine the sugar and water in large pots that they then heat up to 310 degrees Fahrenheit. This is called the hard crack stage. During this stage, the sugar is very malleable and may be poured into molds of different shapes and sizes. Just before the sugar is poured into the molds, coloring and flavoring are added. Once the candy cools, it becomes hard and glass-like.

Write a summary of the passage from *A History of Hard Candy.*

_____

_____

_____

_____

_____

Write a quote from the passage. Remember to give the author credit and put quotation marks around her words.

_____

_____

_____

_____

_____

Write a paraphrase of one idea from the passage. If the information is not common knowledge, give the author credit.

_____

_____

_____

_____

_____

Did you remember to give the author credit and use quotation marks when necessary? Did you avoid plagiarizing? Go back and check your work. Make any corrections that are necessary.

Lesson 13 Taking Notes

As you research, take notes from the sources you read. You should not write down everything you read, but only the information that is most helpful for your report.

Using note cards is a good way to record facts and information. When your notes are complete, you can easily rearrange and organize the cards so that the information flows well and makes sense.

On your note cards, briefly jot down important facts. Write summaries, quotes, or paraphrases that you want to include in your report.

Eric is writing a report on Maine. Here is one of his note cards.

The People

population: about 1.4 million (2000 census)
capital: Augusta
largest cities (in order): Portland, Lewiston, Bangor, Auburn, South Portland, Augusta, Brunswick
"Though the origin of the state's name, Maine, is debated still today, many people believe its name comes from a nautical term."

Maine: A State's Story, pages 14, 17. Monroe, Naomi.

Eric's note card has three important parts. First, at the top he listed the subtopic. He knows that one part of his report will be about the people in the state. He marks each note card with a specific subtopic. Labeling the cards in that way will make organizing them and writing his draft much easier.

Second, Eric wrote his notes. They are very brief. He included facts from the source as well as a quote he might want to use in his report.

Finally, he wrote the title of the source, the author's name, and the page numbers where the information came from. If he needs to go back and check a fact or get more information, he can do it easily.

Lesson 13 Taking Notes

Your assignment is to write a report about a state. You are to include sections on the land, people, history, and business and industry. Find an article about a state of your choice in a print or an online source. Then, take some notes. Label each card with one of the subtopics listed above. Remember to keep your notes brief. Use summaries, quotes, and paraphrases, and write the source at the bottom of each card.

Lesson 14 Using an Outline

An **outline** is a way to organize information. If you are writing a report, writing an outline is an excellent step to take during your prewriting stage. After you collect information and take notes, you can outline the information to make sure you have everything you need.

Eric has begun his outline about Maine.

Maine

I. The Land
    A. Location
        1. bordered on north by Quebec and New Brunswick, Canada
        2. bordered on west by New Hampshire
        3. bordered along southeast by Atlantic Ocean
    B. Regions
        1. White Mountains
        2. New England Upland
        3. Seaboard Lowland
    C. Climate
        1. short summers; long, cold winters
        2. growing season 100–180 days
        3. 36–46 inches rainfall per year
II. The People
    A. Early People
        1. Abnaki
        2. French Canadians

Eric started out with his first subtopic: The Land. Indented under that main idea are three sections: Location, Region, and Climate. Within each section, Eric listed supporting details. Note that this format is called a **topic outline**. The information is recorded in short words and phrases.

Lesson 14 Using an Outline

Look back at the note cards you created on page 89. Create part of an outline from those notes. Go back to the source if you need additional information. Remember, the format and the labels look like this:

I. Main Idea

    A. Topic

        1. Supporting detail

        2. Supporting detail

Lesson 15 Works Cited

The last page of a report is a **Works Cited** page, or a list of the sources used. This bibliography shows readers what sources you used and allows them to consult those sources if they want further information. It also shows your teacher that you used a variety of sources and made good choices.

On a Works Cited page, you need to give certain specific information so that another person could locate that same source. Each type of source has a slightly different format. Here are examples of bibliographic entries for the most common types of sources. If, for any entry, you don't have a piece of information, just skip it and go on to the next piece of information. Pay close attention to punctuation. Periods, commas, quotation marks, and underlining are all part of the format.

Encyclopedia (print or online)

"Title of Article." <u>Title of Encyclopedia</u>. Edition. Year published. Medium of publication.

Example:

"Maine." <u>Encyclopaedia Britannica</u>. 15th edition. 2003. Print.

Book

Author last name, first name. <u>Title of Book</u>. Place of Publication: Publisher, date of publication. Medium of publication.

Example:

Pendleton, Tom. <u>Maine: A State's Story</u>. Portland: Maine State Historical Society, 2004. Print.

Magazine article

Author last name, first name. "Title of Article." <u>Title of Magazine</u>. Day Month Year: page numbers of article. Medium of publication.

Example:

Swift, Marcy. "Portland's Heritage." <u>Travel Maine</u>. 14 June 2005: 34–38. Print.

Web site

Author last name, first name (if given). "Title of Article or Page." <u>Name of Web site</u>. Day Month Year the page was published. Web. Day Month Year you visited the site.

Example:

Altman, Angela. "Maine in June." <u>Portland Visitors' Organization</u>. 21 April 2005. Web. 3 March 2014.

Lesson 15 Works Cited

Now, create bibliographic entries of your own. Locate one or more sources of each type. They don't all have to be about the same topic. What's important is that you practice using the format for each type of source.

Encyclopedia

_____

_____

_____

_____

Book

_____

_____

_____

_____

Magazine article

_____

_____

_____

_____

Web site

_____

_____

_____

_____

Lesson 16 Graphics and Visual Aids

What is a picture worth? If you're putting together a bike, a picture to go along with the instructions can make the difference between success and failure. Sometimes, words can only do so much. Then, you need a picture to help out. Pictures can be drawings, photographs, maps, graphs, or diagrams.

The visual aid below shows a great deal of information, which saves the writer a lot of work.

A recent news article criticized the amount of money that Jennings County Schools spends on fuel and transportation. It is a fact that we spend 15% more on fuel and transportation than neighboring school districts. The reason is because our school district covers a wider area than most other school districts.

Graph the data below to help the Jennings County school superintendent prove that Jennings County has more students than nearby schools and, therefore, needs more money for school lunches. Use a bar graph similar to the one above.

School District	Enrollment
Jennings Co.	25,494 students
Emerson	17,239 students
Tri-Valley	16,117 students
Rock Co.	22,876 students

Lesson 16 Graphics and Visual Aids

A bar graph is just one way to show information in a visual way. Diagrams, circle graphs, and pictographs are also good tools. Here is a visual aid that shows how much money has been raised to build a new building for the humane society.

Now, create your own visual aid. Imagine that your class collected more canned food than several other classes for the school food drive. Think about how you could show that information in a creative and meaningful way. Make up data and write it in this space.

Now, create your visual aid here.

Lesson 17 The Writing Process: Informational Writing

Writing a report is a good way to show what you know. It is also a good way to learn about a topic that interests you. Use the writing process to plan and write a report.

Prewrite

Look back at the topic ideas you recorded on page 83. Which one seems most interesting? Choose one and begin to explore that topic with the help of this chart.

Topic: _____

What I Know	What I Want to Know	How or Where I Might Find Out Information

If you are comfortable with your topic, conduct some research and take notes from a variety of sources. Write summaries, quotes, and paraphrases you may want to use in your report. On each note card, include a subtopic, the source title, and the author's name.

Lesson 17 The Writing Process: Informational Writing

Now, it is time to focus on putting ideas in order. Think about your topic. How should information be organized? By cause and effect? By comparing and contrasting? By spatial organization? Looking at and organizing your note cards might help you decide. List your main points or ideas in order on this page.

[ ]

[ ]

[ ]

[ ]

[ ]

[ ]

Lesson 17 The Writing Process: Informational Writing

Draft

Write a first draft of your report in the space below or in a computer document. Keep your notes and the chart on page 97 nearby as you write. Make sure to give the authors of sources credit and use quotation marks when necessary to avoid plagiarizing. Your writing should be formal in style like Ashley's writing on page 82. For now, don't worry about misspelling words or getting everything perfect. Just get your ideas down in sentences and paragraphs.

Lesson 17 The Writing Process: Informational Writing

Revise

Every writer can improve his or her work. Pick up your report and read it as if you are seeing it for the first time. Remember, even experienced writers feel that revising is much more difficult than writing the first draft.

Answer the questions below about your draft. If you answer "no" to any of these questions, those areas might need improvement. Feel free to make marks on your draft, so you know what needs more work. Ask a friend to read your draft and answer the questions, too.

- Did you present information clearly and in a logical order?

- Does each paragraph consist of a main idea supported by facts?

- Did you include transition words to connect ideas?

- Did you begin with a sentence that will make readers want to keep going?

- Did you use information from several different sources?

- Did you draw a conclusion based on the information presented?

- Did you keep your audience in mind by asking yourself what they might already know or what they need to know?

- Did you give the author credit and use quotation marks when necessary to avoid plagiarism?

Here are a few pointers about making your report interesting to read.

- Vary the length of your sentences. Mixing short, medium, and long sentences keeps your readers interested.

- Vary the style of your sentences. Begin sentences with different kinds of words or clauses. For example, begin some sentences with verbs, some with phrases, and some with clauses.

- Think about a visual aid that will help your readers understand your report. Include it in your revision.

Write a revision of your report on page 100, or make changes to your computer document. As you write, pay special attention to the length and style of your sentences.

Lesson 17 The Writing Process: Informational Writing

_____

_____

_____

_____

_____

_____

_____

_____

_____

_____

_____

_____

_____

_____

_____

_____

_____

_____

_____

_____

_____

_____

_____

_____

_____

_____

_____

_____

_____

_____

_____

_____

Lesson 17 The Writing Process: Informational Writing

Proofread

Now is the time to correct those last little mistakes. Proofreading is easier if you look for just one kind of error at a time. Read through once for capital letters. Read again for end punctuation, spelling, and so on. Use this checklist as you proofread your report. Ask a friend to proofread your report and use the checklist, too.

____ Each sentence begins with a capital letter.

____ Each sentence states a complete thought and ends with the correct punctuation (period, question mark, or exclamation point).

____ All proper nouns begin with capital letters.

____ All words are spelled correctly.

Use standard proofreading symbols as you proofread your revised report.

Remember to read your writing out loud during the proofreading stage. You may hear a mistake or awkward spot that you did not see.

- $\underline{\underline{c}}$apitalize this letter.
- Add a missing end mark: ⊙ ? !
- Add a comma‸please.
- Fix incoᵣrect or misspelled words.
- ~~Delete~~ this word.
- Lowercase this ⁄Letter.

Publish

Write a final copy of your report on separate sheets of paper or make final changes to your computer document. Write or type carefully so there are no mistakes. The final page of your report should be a Works Cited page. Include a title page and a visual aid. Read your report out loud to your class at school or e-mail it to someone who will be interested in your topic.

Chapter 3

Lesson 1 Persuasive Writing

You see persuasive writing every day. You may not even be aware of it. A bus passes by with a sign on its side. In your favorite magazine, you read the letters to the editor. In the school newspaper, a fellow student has written an article about the proposed changes in class offerings for next year. Whatever the form that persuasive writing takes, the writer's goal is to try to make readers think, feel, or act in a certain way.

Here is an example of a persuasive article. The writer gives some information and states her opinion. She closes with a statement that requests some of her readers to take action.

New Classes: Change for the Better?

Times are changing. At least, that's what next year's class list seems to indicate. As of next fall, some classes will never again be offered at OMS.

The home economics department will see drastic changes. Traditional cooking classes are a thing of the past. Instead, students will take a class called *consumer science*. The former home economics rooms will house three new computer labs plus a video lab. Proposed class offerings involve creating multimedia presentations, manipulating digital images, conducting online research, and more.

My question is this: Don't we need to learn how to cook anymore? Maybe it's old-fashioned, but everyone needs to eat. With parents working full-time jobs these days, they have less time to teach us those skills. I like the idea of the new computer offerings, but I don't believe it was the best idea to do away with the basics. Unless people want to rely on fast-food restaurants or convenience foods, cooking is pretty important, I think. I hope the school administrators will reconsider the plan and continue to offer cooking classes.

By Mariah Wayne

It is a good idea to be aware of persuasive writing. For a few days, keep track of the things you see that include persuasive writing. Record them here.

_____   _____

_____   _____

_____   _____

_____   _____

_____   _____

_____   _____

_____   _____

Lesson 1 Persuasive Writing

Do you think it's important to have a cooking class in middle school? Do you think those skills are no longer necessary? Respond to Mariah's article on page 102. State your opinion and support it with reasons. Assume that your article will appear in the school newspaper. Make sure that your opinion is clear and that readers understand what you want them to think or do. How persuasive can you be?

_____

_____

_____

_____

_____

_____

_____

_____

_____

_____

_____

_____

_____

_____

_____

_____

_____

_____

_____

_____

_____

_____

_____

_____

_____

_____

Lesson 2 Facts and Opinions

Which of these sentences below is a fact? Which is an opinion? If you're not sure, ask yourself these questions: Which statement could be proven true? That would be a **fact**. Which is a belief or a personal judgment? That would be an **opinion**.

Cooking classes are no longer offered in many schools.

Cooking classes are a vital part of a middle school education.

Often, writers state both facts and opinions. That is okay, but writers and readers both must be able to tell the difference between the two. Look for facts and opinions as you reread Mariah's article.

New Classes: Change for the Better?

Times are changing. At least, that's what next year's class list seems to indicate. As of next fall, some classes will never again be offered at OMS.

The home economics department will see drastic changes. Traditional cooking classes are a thing of the past. Instead, students will take a class called *consumer science*. The former home economics rooms will house three new computer labs plus a video lab. Proposed class offerings involve creating multimedia presentations, manipulating digital images, conducting online research, and more.

My question is this: Don't we need to learn how to cook anymore? Maybe it's old-fashioned, but everyone needs to eat. With parents working full-time jobs these days, they have less time to teach us those skills. I like the idea of the new computer offerings, but I don't believe it was the best idea to do away with the basics. Unless people want to rely on fast-food restaurants or convenience foods, cooking is pretty important, I think. I hope the school administrators will reconsider the plan and continue to offer cooking classes.

By Mariah Wayne

Use the persuasive writings you found and recorded on page 102. List some facts and opinions they contain.

Facts: _____

_____

_____

_____

_____

Opinions: _____

_____

_____

_____

_____

Lesson 2 Facts and Opinions

Words such as *think, believe, should, must, never, always, like, hate, best,* and *worst* may signal that a statement is an opinion. Scan Mariah's article again and circle any opinion signal words you find.

Write two facts from the article on page 104.

_____

_____

Write two opinions from the article.

_____

_____

One of Mariah's classmates has written her own opinion about the new classes at OMS. Read Tisha's paragraph and look for opinion signal words.

> I think it's about time this school got into the 21st century. At last, we have some decent computer classes. The old cooking classes were always useless. Who can't microwave a frozen waffle? The new classes will teach us to create and use digital images in all sorts of ways. That is a much more useful skill than cooking. I look forward to the new classes and believe that everyone will be better off.

Write one fact from Tisha's paragraph.

_____

_____

Circle any opinion signal words that you find in Tisha's paragraph. Then, write one opinion that Tisha states.

_____

_____

Now, state your own opinion about cooking class versus computer classes. Which do you think is more valuable?

_____

_____

_____

_____

Lesson 3 Emotional Appeals

How do writers get readers to think, feel, or act in a certain way when they write persuasively? Often, they appeal to readers' emotions. When writers make an **emotional appeal**, they try to get at something about which readers feel strongly. For example, Ms. Martinez, the home economics teacher, thinks cooking classes are important. She included this statement in a letter to the editor:

> Our job is to prepare students for life beyond school. Computers and computer classes are available to students in many ways. Cooking classes, however, are available to students only while they are in middle school. If we don't offer cooking classes, we are not doing our jobs.
> Ms. Martinez

Ms. Martinez knows that most people feel strongly about doing their jobs well. She also knows that many people feel strongly about education and about their local schools. Though the statements are opinions (rather than facts), they have a strong emotional appeal and may persuade some readers to believe as the writer does.

Many people have strong feelings about positive issues such as these:

justice	family	security	education
money	home	safety	conservation

People may also have strong feelings toward negative issues such as these:

injustice	crime	waste
violence	pollution	danger

Name some issues about which you have strong feelings.

_____ _____ _____

_____ _____ _____

_____ _____ _____

Emotional appeals may tie into readers' strong feelings about positive or negative issues. Read the letter to the editor on the next page. What kind of emotional appeal does the writer make?

Lesson 3 Emotional Appeals

Dear Editor:

In Lora Webb's article (May 23) about the middle school, she mentions that woodworking class will no longer be offered. I took that class in 1995. My teacher, Mr. Harker, taught me it was okay that I wasn't an "A" student. He also taught me valuable skills, such as planning ahead and sticking with a job until it's done. During high school, I got a part-time job in a furniture factory. I almost dropped out of high school, but I knew my boss would fire me if I quit school. So I stuck with it. After high school, I got a full-time job at another factory. I improved my skills and am now able to work for myself as a cabinetmaker. Without the skills I learned from Mr. Harker in woodworking class, I'm pretty sure I would have become a high school dropout. I know that computers are important in my business, but I wonder if those new computer classes will teach kids any skills that are half as valuable as the ones I learned in woodworking class.

N. Scariffe, Andersonville

Explain the emotional appeal in Mr. Scariffe's letter to the editor.

_____

_____

_____

_____

Write a letter to the editor in response to Mr. Scariffe's letter. Write in support of his opinion or indicate why you disagree with him. Remember to consider your audience. What kind of emotional appeal might make people agree with you?

Dear Editor:

_____

_____

_____

_____

_____

_____

_____

_____

_____

_____

_____

_____

_____

_____

_____

_____

Lesson 4 Advertising

Ready Printing Co.

**Reliable.
On time.
Comfortable.**

If you are a very persuasive writer, you might consider a job writing advertisements. Advertising copywriters rely heavily on emotional appeals to win over customers. They know that people have strong feelings about wanting to feel good, to fit in, and to have fun. Advertisements constantly send messages that writers think people want to hear.

Look at the Ready Printing Co. logo. What does the word *comfortable* have to do with using a printing company?

_____

_____

What message does the drinking water slogan send?

_____

_____

Advertising copywriters know that thinking about audience is especially important. Perhaps the most often-asked questions are these: Who might buy this product? What kind of advertising message can persuade them to buy?

Suppose you are writing an advertisement for a child's car seat. Who is your audience?

_____

_____

To which strong feelings do you need to appeal to get this audience to buy your car seats?

_____

_____

On Your Own Make up a slogan for your city. The slogan should make residents feel proud of their city and should make people want to visit your city.

Lesson 5 Facts, Opinions, and Bias

You already know what facts and opinions are. Facts can be proven to be true. Opinions are judgments that people make. What about bias?

Bias is an unfair "slant" that a writer gives to a topic. Some writers may do it by accident. Perhaps they have such strong views that they don't realize they are presenting only one point of view or only a portion of the facts. Other writers bias their work on purpose to present their own views and to persuade others to believe as they do.

Can you find the bias—the unfair slant—in this portion of a review article about sewing machines?

> This year's new sewing machine models all offer similar features. The SewGood 207T, with a colorful array of buttons, is dizzying in its options. The heavy Marvel XD looks plain by comparison, though it has the same mind-numbing selection of features. One has to look for them on an LCD screen. The EverSeam 1601 looks just like your mother's machine, but has all the features you want for today's fabrics and projects.

The first sentence tells us that all the machines have "similar features." However, the first is "dizzying," and the second is "heavy," "plain," and "mind-numbing." The third, however, is "just like your mother's machine." A reader certainly comes away thinking that the third machine is the best of the bunch.

How could this writer have avoided bias? Consider some replacements for the words that send negative messages. For example, she could have used *dazzling* instead of *dizzying*. For the second model, she could have omitted *heavy* and used *vast array* instead of *mind-numbing selection*. Can you think of other changes that would remove bias from the review? Write them here.

Original Word or Phrase

_____

_____

_____

_____

Replacement Word or Phrase

_____

_____

_____

_____

Lesson 5 Facts, Opinions, and Bias

It is important for readers to recognize bias when they see it. Advertisements often include bias, which is one method of persuasion. News stories might contain bias, which could lead readers to misunderstand an issue. It is important to think about what is fact and what is opinion, and to ask whether all sides of an issue are being fairly presented. As a writer, you should ask the same questions.

Suppose that you are to review some products. You might compare two cell phones, two versions of a video game, or two recordings by your favorite group. Write a fair, unbiased review of the products. Tell what is both good and bad about each product. Remember, in a review, your job is not only to say what you like but to evaluate the products. In the evaluation, you should state both facts, such as "The new model has more features than the old model," and opinions, such as "I find the old model's screen easier to read."

_____

_____

_____

_____

_____

_____

_____

_____

_____

_____

_____

_____

_____

_____

_____

_____

_____

_____

_____

_____

Lesson 6 Order of Importance

When you write about events, you use time order. When you describe a place, you use spatial order. When you write to persuade, a good strategy is to use order of importance.

Remember, when writers write to persuade, they try to make their readers think or act in a certain way. For example, you might try to persuade your principal to offer a Spanish class. As you persuade, you should save your most important ideas—your strongest arguments—for last. Build your ideas from least important to most important.

Here is part of a letter that Alissa wrote to her principal. Notice the reasons she gives for offering a Spanish class at her school.

> Spanish would be a valuable addition to our school's course offerings. The need to speak and understand Spanish increases as the Hispanic population in the United States increases. Improved communication will help English-speaking and Spanish-speaking communities get along. Many jobs and opportunities are available for people who speak both English and Spanish. Educators agree that the best time to learn a language is when you are young. Statistics also indicate that learning a language can teach skills that transfer to other classes, resulting in better grades and test scores.

Alissa gave several reasons for why there should be a Spanish class at her school. Write them in order below from least important to most important.

_____

_____

_____

_____

_____

_____

_____

_____

Lesson 6 Order of Importance

What class do you think your school should add to its course offerings? Decide on a new class, then write a letter to your teacher or principal. Try to persuade the person that your idea is a good one. Ask yourself this: What will make this person want to support my idea?

Before you begin drafting your letter, write your reasons here. Then, number them in the order in which you will use them in your letter. Save the strongest argument, or the most important reason, for last.

Reason: _____

Reason: _____

Reason: _____

Reason: _____

Dear _____ ,

Lesson 7 Writing About Problems and Solutions

Problem and solution is another way to organize persuasive writing. Using this strategy, a writer identifies a problem, gives facts about possible solutions for the problems, and gives an opinion about which solution is best. When Eric studied Maine for his social studies class, he learned that one of Maine's native woodland birds, the whippoorwill, is a threatened species. He decided to write a problem and solution essay about the whippoorwill. He made this chart as part of his prewriting.

Problem:
Whippoorwill populations are decreasing due to loss of their woodland habitat.

↓

Possible solutions:
1. Stop destroying woodland habitat
   control development
2. Set aside some woodland habitat
   woodland preservation
   woodland management

↓

Recommended solution:
Educate people about the importance of preserving woodland habitat. It is the only habitat in which these birds can survive.

When Eric writes his essay, he will state the whippoorwill's problem. Then, he will explore possible solutions, giving facts and evidence to support each one. Finally, he will make a convincing argument that persuades the reader to agree with his opinion about which solution is the best one.

Lesson 7 Writing About Problems and Solutions

Think of a topic that interests you. It might be about an animal species that is disappearing, like the whippoorwill. Or it could be a local issue, such as pollution or the possible destruction of a historic building. Complete the problem-solution chart on this page.

Problem:

↓

Possible solutions:

↓

Recommended solution:

Lesson 8 Identifying and Making a Claim

What is a **claim**? A claim is the main opinion or argument in persuasive writing. The writer's job is to persuade the reader to agree with her or his claim. Claims that are supported with good reasons, facts, and other evidence are more persuasive. Sometimes, the claim of a book or essay is stated clearly. Other times, it must be inferred.

Read the paragraph below from *Common Sense* by the famous American revolutionary writer Thomas Paine. Here, Paine makes the claim that Britain will soon be unable to successfully govern the American colonies. While many people at the time agreed that the American colonies should be free of English rule, many others remained loyal to the British king.

As to government matters, it is not in the power of Britain to do this continent justice: The business of it will soon be too weighty, and intricate, to be managed with any tolerable degree of convenience, by a power, so distant from us, and so very ignorant of us; for if they cannot conquer us, they cannot govern us. To be always running three or four thousand miles with a tale or a petition, waiting four or five months for an answer, which when obtained requires five or six more to explain it in, will in a few years be looked upon as folly and childishness — There was a time when it was proper, and there is a proper time for it to cease.

Write Paine's central claim in your own words.

_____

_____

_____

Make an **X** in front of reasons, facts, and evidence that Paine gives to support his claim. Draw a star by the evidence that you find most persuasive.

___ Managing the business of America will soon be too complicated for Britain.

___ The British are too poor to govern the American continent.

___ The British do not fully understand what it means to be an American.

___ Travel between Britain and America by ship is becoming faster and more convenient.

___ It takes too long for important paperwork to travel between the two continents.

___ Britain is too distant from the American colonies to govern them effectively.

Lesson 8 Identifying and Making a Claim

It is the job of readers to decide whether or not they agree with a writer's claim. If the writer does not provide enough good evidence, they may disagree. Facts often make the best persuasive evidence. However, emotional appeals can be convincing, too.

Read the passage below. Look for a central claim and supporting evidence.

> All children should have free access to candy. Currently, most children have to wait until birthdays or holidays to receive candy. This is unfair because children do not get to eat candy often enough. Most children love candy, and it makes them happy to eat it. It is a good reward for doing homework and other chores. There are so many varieties of candy that it would take years to try them all. Young children cannot go to the store all by themselves to get candy. Kids deserve treats after working hard at school all day. They deserve candy.

What is the writer's claim?

_____

What evidence given to support the claim is convincing?

_____

_____

_____

What evidence given to support the claim is not convincing?

_____

_____

_____

Do you agree or disagree with the claim?

_____

What evidence could you add to make the claim more persuasive?

_____

_____

_____

On Your Own Choose a paragraph from a nonfiction book you have read. Does the author make a central claim? What evidence is given to support the claim? Which evidence is most convincing?

Lesson 9 The Writing Process: Argument

Use the writing process to plan and write a persuasive argument.

Prewrite

Think of an issue you have a strong opinion about. It could be about school lunches, allowances, free time, school dances or other social events, recycling, a problem in a faraway part of the world, or an endangered species that needs protection. It is up to you! Write your opinions about several issues on the lines below.

_____

_____

_____

_____

_____

Which opinion do you care about the most? About which do you want to make a claim and write an argument? Draw a star beside the topic you choose.

Now, fill in the idea web below to collect and organize evidence to support your claim. You may state opinions, but you must also give convincing facts and reasons. Ask an adult to help you find good Web sites or books that will have information to support your claim. As you look for evidence, think about your audience. Who do you want to convince? What facts and evidence will be most persuasive for these readers? Add more ovals to the idea web if you need to.

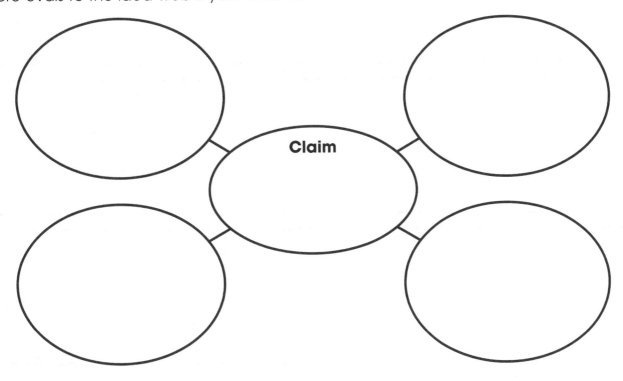

Lesson 9 The Writing Process: Argument

It is time to organize the information you gathered. Use order of importance to order your evidence. What is your strongest piece of evidence? Save that one for last. Write your reasons and supporting evidence in the boxes below. Number them in order.

Lesson 9 The Writing Process: Argument

Draft

Write a first draft of your argument below or type it in a computer document. Refer to your chart on page 118 as you write. Include an introduction that states your claim clearly. In the body of your argument, explain your reasons and evidence connected by transition words. Finally, include a conclusion that makes a final, convincing argument for your claim. As you write, don't worry about spelling or punctuation. Just get your ideas down in sentences and in order.

Lesson 9 The Writing Process: Argument

Revise

Even the most experienced writers read over their work and make changes. If possible, set your writing aside for a few hours. Then, reread your work slowly and carefully. Answer the questions below about your draft. If you answer "no" to any of these questions, those areas might need improvement. Feel free to make marks on your draft, so you know what needs more work. Ask a friend to read your draft and answer the questions, too.

- Did you state your claim clearly in the introduction?

- Did you give strong reasons and facts to support your claim?

- Did you use reliable sources?

- Did you organize your reasons from least important to most important?

- Did you consider your audience?

- Did you write a strong conclusion?

Think carefully about your audience. With persuasive writing, it is especially important to aim your arguments at a specific audience. Ask yourself these questions.

- What opinions does my audience already hold about this issue?

- What does my audience already know about this issue?

- What will they need to know in order to understand the issue?

- What emotional appeals might sway the audience to agree with me?

It is always a good idea to read your work out loud at the revising stage. You might hear awkward sentences or ideas that don't flow quite right.

Write your revised argument on separate sheets of paper or make changes to your computer document. As you revise, remember to keep your audience in mind.

Lesson 9 The Writing Process: Argument

Proofread

Now is the time to correct any last little mistakes. You will be a better proofreader if you look for just one kind of error at a time. Read through once for capital letters. Read again for end punctuation, spelling, and so on. Here is a checklist to use as you proofread your argument. Ask a friend to read your argument and use the checklist, too.

_____ Each sentence begins with a capital letter.

_____ Each sentence ends with the correct punctuation (period, question mark, or exclamation point).

_____ Each sentence states a complete thought.

_____ All words are spelled correctly. (If you're not sure, check a dictionary.)

Use standard proofreading symbols as you proofread your argument.

As you proofread, remember to read your writing out loud, even if there is no one to listen. When you read, you may hear mistakes or awkward spots that you did not see.

- $\underline{\underline{C}}$apitalize this letter.
- Add a missing end mark: $_\odot$? !
- Insert a comma‸please.
- Fix incorᵉct or misspelled words.
- ~~Delete~~ this word.
- Lowercase this Ⱡetter.

Publish

Write a final copy of your argument on separate sheets of paper or make final changes to your computer document. Write or type carefully so there are no mistakes. If you used evidence from sources, don't forget to include a Works Cited page at the end. Now, think of a way to share your argument with your audience. Consider e-mailing your writing to the editor of a newspaper or magazine or reading it aloud over the school announcements.

Writer's Handbook

Parts of Speech

A **noun** is a word that names a person, place, or thing. Common nouns name general things. Proper nouns name specific things and always begin with a capital letter.

Common Nouns	Proper Nouns
officer	Sergeant Rhimes
racehorse	Seattle Slew
park	Yellowstone National Park
store	Becker Hardware

A **verb** is an action word. Verbs also show a state of being. Every complete sentence has at least one verb. Verbs show action in the past, in the present, and in the future.

Last week, my team *lost.*
I *was* sad about the loss.
Today, my team *plays* against Sutherland.
Next week, we *will play* at Hinton.

An **adjective** modifies, or describes, a noun or pronoun. Adjectives tell *what kind, how much* or *how many*, or *which one*.

The *brick* building is the Community Center. *(what kind)*
It has *two* entrances. *(how many)*
I usually use *this* entrance. *(which one)*

An **adverb** modifies a verb, an adjective, or another adverb. Adverbs tell *how, when, where*, or *to what degree*.

We planned the parade *carefully*. *(how)*
We chose the date *already*. *(when)*
The parade route will go *there*. *(where)*
We are *completely* prepared. *(to what degree)*

Writer's Handbook

Punctuation

End marks on sentences show whether a sentence is a statement, a command, a question, or an exclamation.

> This sentence makes a statement.
> Make your bed, please.
> Why might you want to ask a question?
> I can't believe how excited you are!

Commas help keep ideas clear.

> In a list or series: The parade had floats, bands, and old cars.
> In a compound sentence: I waved at my dad, but I'm not sure he saw me.
> After an introductory phrase or clause: After the parade, we all had ice cream.
> To separate a speech tag: I said to Dad, "Did you see me?"

Quotation marks show the exact words that a speaker says. They enclose the speaker's words and the punctuation that goes with the words.

> "Sure, I saw you," Dad said. "How could I have missed that red hat?"
> "That's exactly why I wore it," I said.

Colons are used to introduce a series, to set off a clause, for emphasis, in time, and in business letter greetings.

> My favorite vegetables include the following: *broccoli, red peppers, and spinach. (series)*
>
> The radio announcer said: *"The game is postponed due to rain." (clause)*
>
> The skiers expected the worst as they got off the mountain: *an avalanche. (emphasis)*

Writer's Handbook

The Writing Process

When writers write, they take certain steps. Those steps make up the writing process.

Step 1: Prewrite

First, writers choose a topic. Then, they collect and organize ideas or information. They might write their ideas in a list. They might also make a chart and begin to put their ideas in some kind of order.

Tomika is going to write about her dance lessons. She put her ideas in a web.

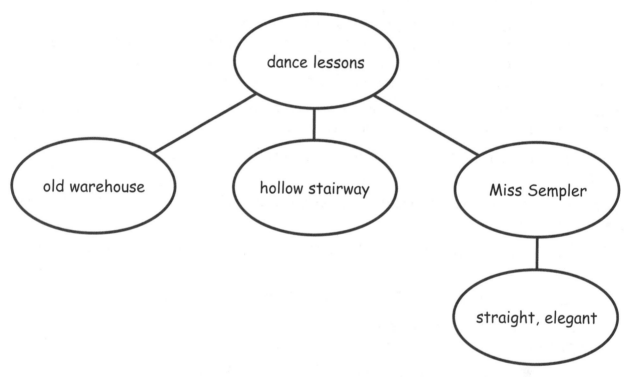

Step 2: Draft

Next, writers put their ideas on paper in a first draft. Writers know that there might be mistakes in this first draft. That's okay. Here is Tomika's first draft.

> Every Wednesday after school I eagerly climb the hollow stairway of the old Benson's Warehouse building I am glad to go dance lessons, even if they are in an old warehouse. Miss Sempler always greets the other students and me. She is so straight and elagant. She says we sound like a heard of hippoes coming up the stairs. I try to go up the stairs with my head high and my shoulders back, just like miss Sempler would.

Writer's Handbook

Step 3: Revise

Then, writers change or fix their first draft. They might decide to move ideas around or to add information. They might also take out words or sentences that don't belong. Here are Tomika's changes.

> Every Wednesday after school I eagerly climb the hollow, echoing stairway of the old Benson's Warehouse building I am glad to go to dance lessons, even if they are in an old warehouse. Miss Sempler always greets the other students and me. She is so straight and elagant. She says we sound like a heard of hippoes coming up the stairs. I try to go up the stairs with my head high and my shoulders back, just like miss Sempler would. I almost feel like a dancer even before I get to class.

Step 4: Proofread

Writers usually write a new copy so their writing is neat. Then, they read again to make sure everything is correct. They read for mistakes in their sentences. Tomika found several more mistakes when she proofread her work.

> Every Wednesday after school, I eagerly climb the hollow, echoing stairway of the old Benson's Warehouse building. I am glad to go to dance lessons, even if they are in an old warehouse. Miss Sempler always greets the other students and me at the top of the stairs. She is so straight and elagant. She says we sound like a heard of hippoes coming up the stairs. I try to go up the stairs with my head high and my shoulders back, just like miss Sempler would. I almost feel like a dancer even before I get to class.

Step 5: Publish

Finally, writers make a final copy that has no mistakes. They are now ready to share their writing with a reader. They might choose to read their writing out loud. They can also add pictures and create a book. There are many ways for writers to publish, or to share, their work with readers.

Writer's Handbook

Personal Narrative

In a personal narrative, a writer writes about something he has done or seen. A personal narrative can be about anything, as long as the writer is telling about one of his or her own experiences. Here is the final version of Tomika's paragraph about dance lessons.

Words that tell time indicate when something happens.	Every Wednesday after school, I eagerly climb the hollow, echoing stairway of the old Benson's Warehouse building. I am glad to go to dance lessons, even if they are in an old warehouse. Miss Sempler always greets the other students and me at the top of the stairs. She is so straight and elegant. She says we sound like a herd of hippos coming up the stairs. I try to go up the stairs with my head high and my shoulders back, just like Miss Sempler would. I almost feel like a dancer even before I get to class.	The words *I* and *me* show that the writer is part of the action.
Describing words and figurative language help readers "see" or "hear" what is happening.		The writer stayed on topic. All of the sentences give information about Tomika's dance lesson.

Descriptive Writing

When writers describe, they might tell about an object, a place, or an event. They use sensory words so that readers can see, hear, smell, feel, or taste whatever is being described. In this example of descriptive writing, Brad described the results of his science experiment.

The writer uses the whole-to-whole comparison method. He describes one plant in this paragraph, and the other plant in the next paragraph.	Daisy plant A was my control plant. It received the same amount of water as plant B, but it received no Epsom salts. Plant A has 9 leaves and is 12.5 inches tall. Its leaves are bright green, and it has a healthy appearance. Daisy plant B received two doses of Epsom salts. The first dose was administered just as the first leaves appeared, and the second was administered one week later. Plant B has 14 leaves and is 14 inches tall. This plant also has 2 flower buds. The leaves are a deep green, and the plant is fuller and has a more pleasing appearance than does daisy plant A.	Sensory details help readers visualize the scene.
		The writer gives information in the same order in each paragraph.

Writer's Handbook

Fiction Stories

Writers write about made-up things. They might write about people or animals. The story might seem real, or it might seem unreal, or fantastic. Here is a story that Jason wrote. It has human characters, and the events could really happen, so Jason's story is realistic.

The story has a beginning, a middle, and an end.		The first paragraph establishes the setting.

Bitter Victory

Coach had put Neil out on the field. He hadn't played all season. Neil suspected that Coach felt sorry for him, but he was glad to be in the game. Not that he figured anything would actually happen. But then, there was the ball. A Hampton player had fumbled it, and fumbled it badly. It was skittering crazily across the chewed-up grass. Now, it was coming right at him.

Neil picked up the ball and looked frantically all around him. There was a lot of confusion. Without his realizing it, Neil's feet were moving. No one was taking much notice. He crouched down a little to hide the ball tucked under his arm. He made his feet go faster and headed for the end zone. He gritted his teeth, expecting to get clobbered. Forty…thirty…twenty…ten…*Whumpf*!

A Hampton player caught him at the last moment. The impact sent Neil careening forward. He stumbled over the line, completely out of control. A sting in his ankle was quickly forgotten; Neil tasted dirt and grass as he rolled and finally came to a stop. Grinning at his approaching teammates, Neil yelled, "We won! We won!"

Neil's teammates were all yelling at him, but not about winning the game. Neil looked down at his ankle, which was bent at a nauseating angle. A blur of noises and movements occurred as Neil was loaded onto a stretcher and carried off. What he remembered, though, was the scoreboard, and the fact that the crowd went wild, just like in the movies.

This story is written in third-person point of view. The narrator is not a part of the action. So, words such as *he, she, her, him,* and *they* refer to the characters.

Sensory words help readers visualize what is happening.

Time and order words keep ideas clear.

Informational Writing

When writers write to inform, they present information about a topic. Informational writing is nonfiction. It is not made up; it contains facts. Here is a paragraph from a report about the Olympics.

The writer states the main idea in a topic sentence. It is the first sentence of the paragraph.

The Olympics

The tradition of the Olympics is a long and honorable one. The first Olympics were played in Greece more than 2,500 years ago. The initial contest was held in 776 B.C. There was just one event—a footrace. Later, the Greeks added boxing, wrestling, chariot racing, and the pentathlon. The ancient Games were held every four years for more than a thousand years.

These sentences contain details that support the main idea.

A time-order word connects ideas.

Writer's Handbook

Explanatory (or How-to) Writing

When writers explain how to do things, they might tell how to make a craft, play a computer game, or use a cell phone. Tony has written instructions for Jenna, who is going to take care of Tony's hamster while he is on vacation.

The first sentence summarizes the care instructions.	Each day when you come, there are three things to do. First check Heidi's water to make sure the bottle hasn't fallen out of place. Then fill her food dish. Her food is in the green bag next to the cage. Finally play with Heidi. She would love to snuggle in your neck and maybe crawl down your sleeve.

Order words help readers keep the steps in order.

Clear words help readers understand the instructions.

Persuasive Writing

In persuasive writing, writers try to make readers think, feel, or act in a certain way. Persuasive writing shows up in newspaper and magazine articles, letters to the editor, business letters, and, of course, advertisements. Trina has written a letter to the editor of her school newsletter.

The writer begins by stating her opinion.

Dear Editor:
The locker bay is a mess. So many of the lockers are old, scratched, and dented. Some of them don't even close properly. How can we be proud of our school when the locker room is falling apart? More importantly, the worn-out lockers seem to encourage students to mistreat them even further. Someone needs to repair or replace the lockers so that we can feel good about our school.
Trina Hardesty

The writer states facts to lend support to her opinions.

The writer uses an emotional appeal to persuade readers to agree with her.

The writer includes a specific request for action.

Writer's Handbook

Business Letters

Writers write business letters to people or organizations with whom they are not familiar. Business letters usually involve a complaint or a request for information. Mariko needs information for a school report. She wrote a business letter to request information.

The heading includes the sender's address and the date.

8213 Rivera Boulevard
Fredericksburg, TX 78624
March 4, 2015

The inside address is the complete name and address of the recipient.

Dr. Olivia Lamas, DVM
Lamas Animal Clinic
944 Curry Lane
Fredericksburg, TX 78624

Dear Dr. Lamas:

A colon follows the greeting.

My class is exploring careers this month. I would like to learn about being a veterinarian. Is there a time when I can visit your office? I have many questions, and I would like to watch you work with the animals.

The text of the letter is the body.

Please call my teacher, Ms. Zapata, to set up a time that is convenient for you. The school's phone number is 830-555-0021.

Thank you for your help, and I look forward to meeting you.

Sincerely,

A comma follows the closing.

The sender always includes a signature.

Mariko Campillo
Mariko Campillo

Answer Key

Introduction

Lesson 1

Page 6
Order of steps shown:
Step 4: Proofread
Step 5: Publish
Step 1: Prewrite
Step 3: Revise
Step 2: Draft

Lesson 2

Page 7
Possible purposes for writing:
news article—to inform, to explain
personal narrative—to inform, to explain
story—to entertain
business letter—to inform, to persuade

Lesson 3

Page 9
Suggestions may include describing warm-ups, explaining how teams should be picked, the rules or set-up for dodge ball, what freeze tag is, and what "centers" are.
Instructions to substitute teacher will vary.

Lesson 4

Page 10
Details will vary.
Paragraphs will vary.

Page 11
Revised, proofread, and rewritten paragraphs will vary.

Lesson 5

Page 12
Topic sentence: My grandmother is one of those people who has her holiday shopping done by September.

Details:
She picks out gifts when she and Grandpa travel. She goes to local stores when they have good sales during the summer.

Page 13
Possible main idea: Shopping can be annoying.
Paragraphs will vary.

Lesson 6

Page 14
Underlined topic sentence: For a city kid, country life can be a little alarming.
Crossed-out sentence: Possums are not even in the same family as rats.
Details will vary.
Paragraphs will vary.

Lesson 7

Page 16
Steve viewed the exhibit.
X The exhibit was lit with special lights.
Elijah was looking at one display.
X Visitors were entertained by a pianist.
Sentences will vary.

Chapter 1

Lesson 1

Page 17
Possible details:
See: white sleeve, head down, caramel hanging on my chin
Hear: Scruunnch
Smell: rich, sweet caramel
Touch: juices flowed, gooey brown caramel, sticky mess
Taste: juices flowed; rich, sweet caramel; tartness

Answer Key

Page 18
Details and paragraphs will vary.

Lesson 2

Page 19
Possible revised sentence: An impatient
   driver blew his noisy horn.

Page 20
Possible revised sentences:
A driver blows his horn angrily.
The trucks roll noisily to a stop at the
   corner.
The cab of a big truck can be amazingly
   comfortable.
Trucks move goods efficiently across the
   entire country.

Lesson 3

Page 21
Details and paragraphs will vary.

Page 22
Details and paragraphs will vary.

Lesson 4

Page 23
Topic ideas will vary.
Entries in idea webs will vary.

Page 24
Methods of organization and paragraphs
   will vary.

Page 25
Revisions will vary.

Page 26
Published descriptive paragraphs will vary.

Lesson 5

Page 28
Responses to idea-starters will vary.

Lesson 6

Page 29
Time words and phrases will vary.
Sentences will vary.

Page 30
Circled words in paragraph: A week later,
   As soon as, Then
Paragraphs will vary.

Lesson 7

Page 31
Ideas and idea webs will vary.

Page 32
Entries in sequence charts will vary.

Page 33
Drafts will vary.

Page 35
Revisions will vary.

Lesson 8

Page 39
Main character: Morgan
Possible details: He is not on Earth. He is
   on the way to Monroe Flats. He is the
   Environment Manager for a colony.
   He likes to walk. He uses a Telewave to
   communicate.
Other character: the Chairman
Possible details: He speaks in "smooth
   tones." He has Morgan's respect.
Setting: on a planet other than Earth
Possible setting details: quiet, empty,
   craters, hard ground, gray dusty sand
Problem: The main character sees tracks
   and cannot identify their source.
Main character's action: He follows the
   tracks to investigate.
Dialogue (possible answers):
Main character: He speaks respectfully to
   the Chairman.

Answer Key

Other character: The Chairman does not chit-chat; he is business-like.

Sensory details: quietness, "walking on hard ground," "churning and making noise," empty, "gray, dusty sand," "like a person who shies away from a snake," "swishy trail," "smooth tones," buzzing

Lesson 9

Page 40
Titles and settings will vary.

Page 41
Information from passage: The main character has been in this place for 472 days. It's a very quiet place. It is not Earth. The ground is hard, and the character is walking. A colony, which has a generator, is in the distance.
Mood or feeling (possible responses): serious, a "quiet" feeling, thoughtful
Words that convey mood: quietness, empty
Responses will vary.

Lesson 10

Page 42
Characters listed will vary.
"The Colony" character details (possible answers):
The setting is not on Earth—narrator reveals information.
The character's job is to run tests on soil and atmosphere—narrator reveals information.
The main character's name is Morgan—other character's words reveal information.
Morgan respects the Chairman—character's words reveal information.
Morgan is not timid—character's actions reveal information.

Page 43
Responses and paragraphs will vary.

Lesson 11

Page 44
Chairman: He is either excited or angry about Morgan being out alone.
Kip: He respects the Chairman.

Page 45
"I wonder why the Chairman is so upset," said Kip.
The Chairman yelled, "Morgan should never have gone that far out!"
"Is the transport module ready yet?" he asked.
Dialogue will vary.

Lesson 12

Page 47
Responses will vary.

Lesson 13

Page 48
Responses will vary.
Realistic story ideas will vary.

Page 49
Responses will vary.
Science fiction story ideas will vary.

Lesson 14

Page 50
Character details in idea webs will vary.

Page 51
Story maps will vary.

Page 52
Drafts will vary.

Page 54
Revisions will vary.

Answer Key

Chapter 2

Lesson 1

Page 56
Responses will vary.

Page 57
Order words underlined in paragraph: First, As soon as, Then
Responses will vary.

Lesson 2

Page 58
Underlined words in paragraph: First, down, end, bottom, straight, past, Then, right, down, end, left, beyond

Page 59
Directions will vary.

Lesson 3

Page 60
Responses and entries in idea webs will vary.

Page 61
Entries in organizational chart will vary.

Page 62
Instructions will vary.

Page 64
Revisions will vary.

Lesson 4

Page 66
Circled cause-and-effect words: so, as a result
Possible causes and effects:
Cause: Plates rub against each other. Effect: Plates buckle or overlap.
Cause: Plates buckle or overlap. Effect: Surface of Earth shakes or heaves.

Page 67
Possible causes and effects:
Cause: Brian does an emergency landing. Effect: He is hurt and alone.
Cause: Brian builds shelter and makes spears. Effect: He is protected.
Cause: Brian makes spears. Effect: He is able to obtain fish for food.
Cause: Brian uses his wits. Effect: He survives.
Responses will vary.

Lesson 5

Page 68
Circled words in paragraph: because, As a result, Because, Since
Possible causes and effects:
Cause: There was an oil slick. Effect: Marsh's car went out of control.
Cause: Marsh went out of control. Effect: His vehicle left the roadway.
Cause: The guardrail is being replaced. Effect: A temporary guardrail was in place.
Cause: The temporary guardrail did not stop the vehicle. Effect: The vehicle went down an embankment and lodged in a tree.
Cause: The temporary railing did not work. Effect: An investigation will be performed.

Page 69
Responses will vary.
Paragraphs will vary.

Lesson 6

Page 70
Circled spatial words: past, Through, above, Beyond, higher
Spatial descriptions will vary.

Page 71
Descriptive paragraphs will vary.

Answer Key

Lesson 7

Page 72
One bed is lumpier than the other.
That bed must be more uncomfortable than the other.
I would rather sleep on the neater bed.
Sentences will vary.

Page 73
Comparative sentences will vary.
smarter, tallest, happiest, older

Lesson 8

Page 74
Entries in Venn diagrams will vary.

Page 75
Comparisons will vary.

Lesson 9

Page 77
Titles will vary.
Diagrams will vary.

Page 78
Charts will vary.

Page 79
Drafts will vary.
Titles will vary.

Lesson 10

Page 83
Circled transition words (in text on page 82): but, because, so, so, then, Then, and, Next, Finally, then, but
Topic explorations will vary.

Lesson 11

Page 84
Possible responses:
almanac
Web site; online encyclopedia

print encyclopedia
atlas
newspaper
dictionary
online encyclopedia; Web site

Page 85
yes
no
yes
no

Lesson 12

Page 87
Summaries, quotes, and paraphrases will vary.

Lesson 13

Page 89
Entries on note cards will vary.

Lesson 14

Page 91
Outlines will vary.

Lesson 15

Page 93
Bibliographic entries will vary, but must follow the formats given.

Lesson 16

Page 94
Bar graphs will vary.

Page 95
Visual aids will vary.

Lesson 17

Page 96
Entries in chart will vary.

Page 97
Entries in chart will vary.

Answer Key

Page 98
Drafts will vary.

Page 100
Revisions will vary.

Chapter 3

Lesson 1

Page 102
Persuasive examples will vary.

Page 103
Persuasive articles will vary.

Lesson 2

Page 104
Facts and opinions will vary.

Page 105
Circled opinion signal words (in text on page 104): never, like, believe, think, hope
Possible facts from Mariah's article:
Some classes will never again be offered at OMS.; Students will take consumer science.; Former home ec rooms now house computer labs and a video lab.; Proposed class offerings involve multimedia presentations, digital images, online research.; Parents work full-time and have less time to teach cooking skills.
Possible opinions from Mariah's article:
Changes to the home ec department are "drastic."; Cooking is old-fashioned.; It wasn't a good idea to do away with cooking classes.; Cooking is important.
Fact from Tisha's article:
New classes involve creating and using digital images.
Circled opinion signal words: think, always, believe

Possible opinions from Tisha's article:
Students may cite any sentence except the one about the content of the new classes.
Students' personal opinions will vary.

Lesson 3

Page 106
Issues will vary.

Page 107
The emotional appeal in Mr. Scariffe's letter is aimed at strong positive feelings that people have about education and hard work. It also gets at strong feelings people have about people who drop out of school or seem to be "wasting" their education.
Letters to the editor will vary.

Lesson 4

Page 108
Comfortable is how the printing company wants you to feel about using their services.
Just because "other people" are drinking Kool Water, you should, too.
Audience for car seat ad: parents
I would need to appeal to their strong feelings about safety and comfort for their children.

Lesson 5

Page 109
Replacement words or phrases will vary.

Page 110
Product reviews will vary.

Answer Key

Lesson 6

Page 111
Reasons why there should be a Spanish class:
1) It would be a valuable addition to course offerings.
2) The need to speak and understand Spanish increases as the Hispanic population in the United States increases.
3) Improved communication will help English-speaking and Spanish-speaking communities get along.
4) Many jobs and opportunities are available for people who speak both English and Spanish.
5) Educators agree that the best time to learn a language is when you are young.
6) Statistics also indicate that learning a language can teach skills that transfer to other classes, resulting in better grades and test scores.

Page 112
Prewriting notes and letters will vary.

Lesson 7

Page 114
Charts will vary.

Lesson 8

Page 115
Central claim: The British will soon be unable to effectively govern the American colonies.
X Managing the business of America will soon be too complicated for Britain.
X The British do not fully understand what it means to be an American.
X It takes too long for important paperwork to travel between the two continents.
X Britain is too distant from the American colonies to govern them effectively.

Page 116
Claim: All children should have free access to candy.
Evidence cited will vary.
Students' opinions will vary.
Possible additional evidence will vary.

Lesson 9

Page 117
Issues and opinions will vary.
Ideas in idea webs will vary.

Page 118
Charts will vary.

Page 119
Drafts will vary.